The GARDENS of BUNNY MELLON

LINDA JANE HOLDEN

PHOTOGRAPHS BY ROGER FOLEY
FOREWORD BY SIR PETER CRANE

VENDOME

NEW YORK · LONDON

CONTENTS

FOREWORD

The life of Rachel Lambert "Bunny" Mellon spanned almost the entire twentieth century. It was a remarkable life in so many ways, not least in its intersection with the lives of President and Mrs. Kennedy. But it was also a life anchored by deep engagement in the world of plants, gardens, and landscapes. Together with an unerring aesthetic sensibility and the knowledge gleaned from the books of her astonishing personal library, the natural world gave Mrs. Mellon's life meaning. If beauty is the harmonious relationship among parts, then Mrs. Mellon, through the gardens and landscapes she designed, was a creator of beauty. • Rachel Lambert's interest in plants and gardens began at a very young age and from the beginning was inspired and shaped by the magnificent books that she collected. She made her first major rare book purchase, *The Flower-Garden Display'd* by early eighteenth-century British horticulturist Robert Furber, in the early 1920s; it was quickly followed by other acquisitions. "My beginning," she would often say, "started with rare books on plants and garden plans, mostly French or Italian. They were like my bibles."

Before the age of twelve, encouraged by her father, Gerard B. Lambert, and her maternal grandfather, Arthur H. Lowe, Bunny was already a focused participant in designing and maintaining the gardens and grounds at Albermarle, the family estate in Princeton, New Jersey. Later she played an even more assertive role at Carter Hall, her father's new estate in the Shenandoah Valley of northern Virginia. By the 1930s, she had already been commissioned to design gardens for wealthy and influential patrons. These deep, early roots provided structure and support for the lifetime of creativity manifested in the diverse and spectacular gardens featured in this book, from Virginia and Washington, D.C., to New York, Cape Cod, Nantucket, Antigua, and France.

Especially important is the uniquely beautiful walled garden that Mrs. Mellon created at Oak Spring, her home in northern Virginia. With the Blue Ridge Mountains to the west and the Bull Run Mountains to the east, Oak Spring is set in one of the most tranquil and beguilingly beautiful landscapes of North America. We are truly fortunate that this magical place is now the home of the Oak Spring Garden Foundation, which exists to perpetuate and share Mrs. Mellon's marvelous legacy, including her home, garden, estate, and library. Consistent with her wishes, the goal of the foundation is to inspire public engagement and scholarship about the history and future of plants, including the culture of gardens and landscapes and the importance of plants for people.

For those of us fortunate enough to experience Oak Spring every day, it is too easy to take its exquisite beauty for granted. The garden and landscape are welcoming and comfortable. But their seeming informality can be misleading. Mrs. Mellon's designs reflect not only innate talent and exquisite artistic sensibility but also deep and analytical thought. Mrs. Mellon's style is sometimes summarized in her oft-repeated phrase "nothing should be noticed," but equally it was her practice that no detail should be ignored. Her exquisite blending of plants and landscape did not come about by accident. Her gardens, like the interiors that she designed, are purposeful works of art infused with insight from serious study and contemplation, as well as adherence to a few key principles. Distant horizons were a constant reminder to her of the key relationship between land and sky, the importance of the horizontal, and the need for careful attention to lines of sight. Space, light, openness—each a visual metaphor for optimism—were her watchwords.

Throughout her life, but especially during her marriage to Paul Mellon, Mrs. Mellon's strong aesthetic sense also found expression in the artists and designers that she befriended, from Cristóbal Balenciaga and Hubert de Givenchy to Johnny Schlumberger and Diego Giacometti. She was also early in recognizing the genius of Mark Rothko, Richard Diebenkorn, and many others. Equally, and very significantly, she influenced the taste of Paul Mellon, further expanding his lifelong appreciation of art and encouraging him to collect the works of French Impressionists. Together, Mr. and Mrs. Mellon were great collectors and patrons in the world of art, but as this book makes clear, Mrs. Mellon was also an artist in her own right. She expressed her creativity in three dimensions, embracing the challenge of a living palette that changes with the seasons.

In this book, Linda Jane Holden brings together for the first time the brilliant accomplishments of Mrs. Mellon in garden design, and Roger Foley's outstanding photographs capture the essence of some of the very special places that she created. For all of us at the Oak Spring Garden Foundation, it is a pleasure to be able to share their beauty, while also reminding us all of Mrs. Mellon's refined taste and style.

Sir Peter Crane FRS
President
Oak Spring Garden Foundation
osgf.org

Gardens in Virginia

OAK SPRING GARDEN AND FARM

Rachel Lambert was born on August 9, 1910, in New York City, the eldest of Gerard Barnes and Rachel Lowe Lambert's three children. She was nicknamed "Bunny" by a family nurse, and the name stuck. When she was seven years old, the family moved to Albemarle, an eighteen-acre estate in Princeton, New Jersey. • Bunny's earliest memory of the outside world was of a garden. In the preface to *An Oak Spring Sylva*, she recalls "being very small near a bed of tall white phlox in my godmother's garden. This towering forest of scent and white flowers was the beginning of ceaseless interest, passion, and pleasure in gardens and books." She especially enjoyed storybooks and fairy tales, cherishing Beatrix Potter's quaint illustrations of greenhouses and flower pots, Kate Greenaway's equally charming drawings of trees laden with ripened apples, Henriette Willebeek Le Mair's sweet watercolors of gardens in *Little Songs of Long Ago*, and Friedrich de la Motte Fouqué's romantic tale *Undine*.

PAGES 10–11: A view of the complex of stone cottages that comprise Oak Spring, from the southeast.

PAGE 12: Bunny rabbits are often seen nibbling on these grape hyacinths and violets in the Oak Spring garden.

PAGE 13: This illustration, "Little Jumping Joan," from Henriette Willebeek Le Mair's *Little Songs of Long Ago*, was one of Bunny's favorites. She thought that it expressed the freedom she felt when she was in a garden.

LEFT AND BELOW: Bunny's maternal grandfather, Arthur Haughton Lowe, gave her *Flower Guide: Wild Flowers East of the Rockies* to encourage her love of the outside world.

OPPOSITE: Bunny's watercolor of the playhouse and garden she designed and had built on the grounds of Albemarle, the Lambert family home in Princeton, New Jersey.

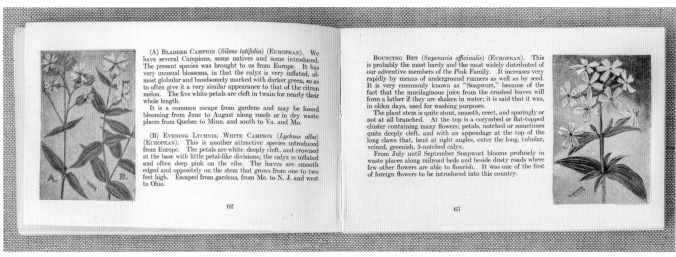

Her maternal grandfather, Arthur Haughton Lowe, encouraged her love of the outside world with books such as Chester A. Reed's *Flower Guide: Wild Flowers East of the Rockies*, and travel, including a trip to Concord, Massachusetts, where he introduced her to the lives and writings of Henry David Thoreau, Nathaniel Hawthorne, and Ralph Waldo Emerson. Emerson's observation "The invariable mark of wisdom is to see the miraculous in the common" became ever more meaningful to her in the years to come.

At Albemarle, Bunny drew inspiration watching the gardeners shape and cultivate the family property. She lined windowsills with small potted plants and planted miniature gardens in spare seed trays found in a greenhouse in an attempt to bring her beloved fairy-tale illustrations to life. "I have gone through all the exciting stages of gardening, beginning with a packet of sweet alyssum and a packet of radishes bought in the country hardware store when I was seven," she wrote in her garden journal.

Her first garden was a fifteen-by-fifteen-foot plot that her father marked off at her request outside the family dining room. Bunny remembered that he would visit her there every day. She told me that a much-admired birdbath was the first item she placed in the garden, followed by a rose bush lifted from her mother's flower bed, and that she just "went from there."

In the preface to *An Oak Spring Pomona*, Bunny wrote, "Children often find their symbols of stability and peace among the daily presence of things they love. For me they were apple trees. The driveway to our house was

lined with apple trees." Mr. Lambert had transplanted old apple trees from a nearby orchard to Albermarle's long driveway. The resulting allée was a showstopper: in spring, the scent of fluffy pink apple blossoms filled the air; in summer, the trees provided welcome shade; in fall, ready-to-pick red and yellow fruit hung from the gnarly branches; and in winter, the bare branches cast blue shadows on the snow. When "leaving early in the morning for school and returning in the afternoon, they were always there to welcome me. I knew their shapes by heart," she wrote.

Mr. Lambert was proud of Bunny, his own young apple who hadn't fallen too far from his tree. She had "exquisite taste and the most original mind of anyone I knew." In his autobiography, *All out of Step: A Personal*

Chronicle, he described her early bent for garden design: "Bunny began to show a talent that she has developed ever since. She designed and had built a small playhouse in the woods near our house in Princeton. She stood over the workmen every minute, directing them. It was of concrete blocks with a thatched roof of straw. It had a Dutch door that opened in two sections and was painted blue. There was a square walled garden in front with tiny boxwood bushes forming intricate patterns, and rare shrubs and vines. Inside, it was completely furnished. Everything there was in the scale of the house. From this first effort came many beautiful gardens, some done as professional jobs. She has this same talent in decorating, and like her father, she loves to do things over. Nothing is ever finished."

On June 3, 1929, Bunny graduated from Foxcroft, a private girls' school in Middleburg, Virginia. Her hands were in the dirt there too. She refurbished the school library's courtyard and refreshed the gardens around campus. After graduation, the father-daughter duo restored the house and grounds at Carter Hall, a historic plantation in Millwood, Virginia, that he had just purchased.

She worked on friends' gardens as well. "One of the first gardens I did outside the family was for the designer Hattie Carnegie," Bunny told Paula Deitz in a 1982 profile that appeared in the *New York Times*. "I was 23 then, and I went to her salon, but could not afford any of her dresses myself, though I loved them. Miss Carnegie suggested I do a garden in exchange for a coat and dress, and so I designed and planted a garden for her." She also created

gardens for French jewelry designer Jean Schlumberger and Charles Ryskamp, a professor of British literature at Princeton who went on to become director of the Pierpont Morgan Library and the Frick Collection.

In the tradition of Thomas Jefferson, Bunny kept a notebook to track experiments. On a page with the heading "Sown Out of Doors—Virginia 1935," she meticulously recorded observations of a favorite white *Phlox drummondii*: "Date of Sowing, June 1; Germination, took ten days to germinate; Bloom date, August 17; Remarks: transplanted successfully. It was very dwarf."

Note taking evolved into garden writing. In 1938 she published "The Garden Plan" in the *Clarke Courier* and shared her exacting method: make a list of everything on the site you don't want—and then make a list of every-

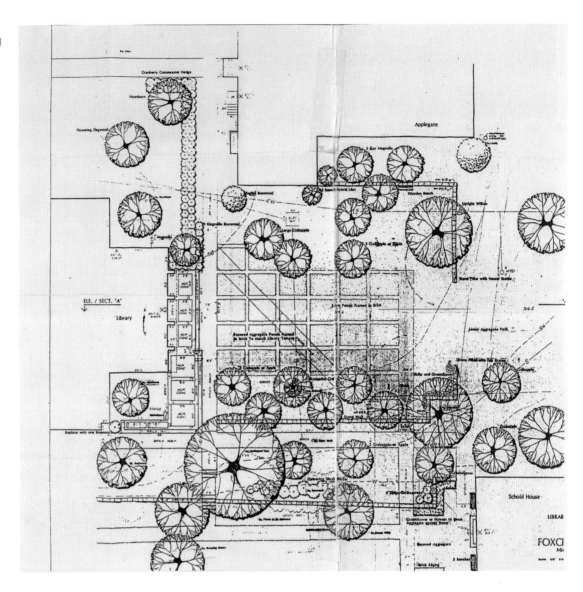

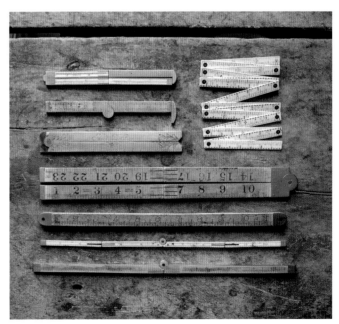

thing you do. Measure it all—the house, the garden paths—"everything you want to know," and write it all down. Among her suggestions: use a blue pencil to outline existing buildings and important trees. Mark the path of the sun. Next, outline all desired improvements with an ordinary pencil (it erases easily), and finally, outline the final plan in red. A list of helpful supplies included graph paper, a ruler, a long measuring tape, some colored pencils, and a good eraser.

With a manual of instructions in one hand and pruning shears in the other, Bunny Mellon's diligence began to pay off. Years later, in *A White House Diary*, Lady Bird Johnson described Bunny as "one of the great authorities on gardens, on planting in general, and a working-at-it authority, a planning, creative, authority."

"Gardening is a way of thinking," Bunny once said. "Landscapes must put together things of nature that correspond to the person as well as the place. It must inspire calm and peace."

During their fifty-one-year marriage, Paul and Bunny Mellon owned houses and gardens in Upperville, Virginia; Cape Cod and Nantucket, Massachusetts; Antigua, in the West Indies; New York City; and Washington, D.C. But the Upperville property, Rokeby, a 4,000-acre farm in the foothills of the Virginia Piedmont, sixty miles west of Washington, D.C., was their favorite. With its gently rolling hills and creeks meandering through green fields, Rokeby was an ideal spot for their favorite pastimes: farming, cattle raising, thoroughbred horse breeding and racing, and gardening.

Paul's father, the banker and industrialist Andrew Mellon (secretary of the Treasury to three U.S. Presidents; U.S. ambassador to the United Kingdom), acquired Rokeby in 1931 for his former wife, Nora McMullen Mellon. At the time it was a 400-acre horse-breeding farm owned by Rear Admiral Cary Grayson, who had served as Woodrow Wilson's physician and later became chairman of the Red Cross.

Paul Mellon and his first wife, Mary Conover Brown, parents of Timothy and Catherine, purchased Rokeby in 1936 from Paul's mother (his father thought it was a poor investment) and over time bought up the adjacent working farms—Edgecliff, Sunridge, Langhorne, Loughborough, and Oak Spring—expanding Rokeby to more than 4,000 acres to accommodate Paul's thoroughbred breeding and racing operations, as well as horseback riding and fox hunting. The Mellons were friendly with Stacy and Rachel (Bunny) Lambert Lloyd, who lived in nearby Clarke County. Bunny gave gardening advice to Mary, and Stacy shared a flat in London with Paul during the war. In 1946 Mary died unexpectedly of an asthma attack. The Lloyds divorced soon thereafter; Bunny Lloyd married Paul Mellon in May 1948 and moved to Rokeby with her two children, Stacy III and Eliza. By 1953, construction had begun on a new Mellon family home amid old oak trees, ponds, and natural springs. The Mellons called their new home Oak Spring.

PAGES 22–23: A fence bordering a lane on the farm casts shadows in the morning light.

PAGE 23 RIGHT: A willow tree by the springhouse, located due south of the main house, in early spring. The roof of the springhouse can be seen in the lower right-hand corner.

PAGES 24–25: The entry drive to the main house passes by a towering beech tree.

TOP LEFT: The Rokeby Farm metes and bounds marker, embedded at the entrance to the house.

BOTTOM LEFT: An Asian pear is espaliered on the stone wall outside Mrs. Mellon's bedroom.

OPPOSITE: The entrance to the main house at Oak Spring.

PAGE 28: The so-called Sunday Kitchen, where Mrs. Mellon "cooked" on the staff's day off. The ceramic tiles are by Martine Vermeulen.

PAGE 29: The axial path in the Formal Garden extends from the patio outside the Sunday Kitchen through three terraces.

PAGES 30–31: A bookcase purchased from Colefax and Fowler in 1948 displays a portion of Bunny's collection of vegetable-shaped and botanical-themed ceramics.

OAK SPRING GARDEN

Oak Spring is a complex of weathered-stone cottages with shingled roofs, connected to one another by a high stone wall. Surrounding a Formal Garden, it resembles an eighteenth-century French hamlet and has the aura of a step back in time. Reached via a drive off Rokeby Road, the stone entryway was referred to by Paul Mellon as "the ruin" because his wife had torn it apart and rebuilt it so many times. A commanding beech, still there today, provided shade near the front door, and a nearby grove of trees was planted with some of Bunny's favorite specimens: catalpa, hawthorn, saucer magnolia, serviceberry, sycamore, and a willow, its long, narrow leaves skimming the surface of a springhouse creek. The twining Virginia creeper that covers the east façade of the main house takes center stage in autumn, when its dull green foliage turns the color of fire. There are many "pricklies," as J. D. Tutwiler, Bunny's gardener for more

than thirty years, calls them, for the birds: hawthorn, holly, and hardy orange—too numerous to count. Bird feeders brimming with seed proliferate throughout the gardens. Keeping the feeders full is at the top of every Oak Spring gardener's to-do list.

The Formal Garden is located in the walled-off area of the complex, overlooked by the back of the main house, just outside the "Sunday Kitchen," where Bunny did the cooking on Sundays so the staff could spend the day with their families. She laid out the garden with a subtlety that adhered to her design ethos: nothing should be noticed; nothing should be obvious. She wanted it to look natural, as though God had created it. Every branch should have its own space; each plant should complement every other; If a plant wandered in, that was just fine. Perfection is achieved in the imperfect.

The garden matured over time, becoming more refined with each passing season and year. Its beauty was in the details. Bunny encouraged her visitors to look for

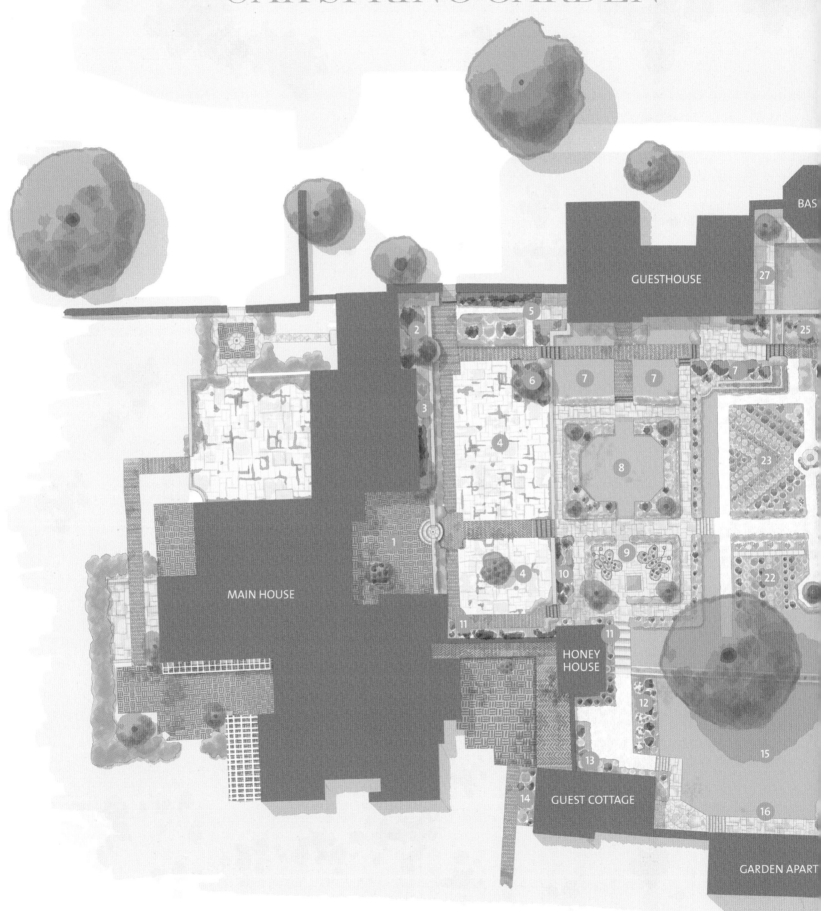

OAK SPRING GARDEN

MAIN HOUSE

GUESTHOUSE

HONEY HOUSE

GUEST COTTAGE

GARDEN APART

BAS

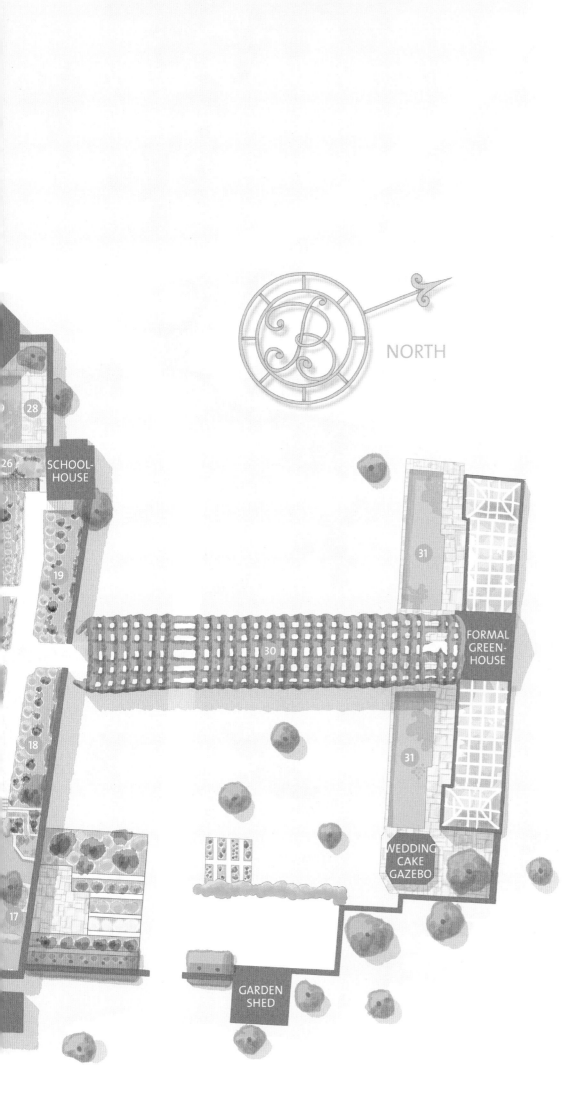

NORTH

GARDEN KEY

1   Sunday Kitchen Patio
2   White Garden
3   Espaliered Holly Bed
4   Upper Terrace
5   Rose Garden
6   Sugar Pear Bed
7   Guesthouse Beds
8   Square Garden
9   Butterfly Garden
10 Tea Garden
11 Honey House Beds
12 South Croquet Lawn Bed
13 Shade Beds
14 Pantry Garden
15 Croquet Lawn
16 East Croquet Lawn Bed
17 North Croquet Lawn Bed
18 East Wall Bed
19 West Wall Bed
20 North Vegetable Garden
21 Herb Garden
22 East Vegetable Garden
23 South Vegetable Garden
24 Flax Bed
25 South Basket House Bed
26 North Basket House Bed
27 South Basket House Patio
28 North Basket House Patio
29 Basket House Reflecting Pool
30 Mary Potter Crab Apple Allée
31 Formal Greenhouse Reflecting Pools

these details; it was part of the rare experience of being invited to see the garden—a privilege extended to a lucky few. The roster of guests included kings and queens (Queen Elizabeth II among them), princes and princesses, presidents and first ladies. No cameras were allowed, so visitors had only their memory to rely on, which caused them to slow their pace, linger along the paths, and appreciate the moment.

The Oak Spring garden can be thought of as three connecting rooms: the Formal Garden, the Allée, and the Formal Greenhouse. The half-acre Formal Garden is divided into three terraces—Upper, Middle, and Lower. An old grindstone embedded in the ground just off the patio at the back of the house marks the beginning of a fifty-two-inch-wide south–north axial path that descends through the terraces, continues through a medieval-style gate, then through a tree-lined canopy of crab apples known as the Allée, and culminates at the Victorian-style Formal Greenhouse.

PAGES 32–33: Plan of the Oak Spring Garden.

PAGE 34 TOP AND BOTTOM: The Sunday Kitchen patio in spring and summer.

PAGE 35: A millstone is embedded in the steps leading down from the Sunday Kitchen patio to the Upper Terrace.

PAGES 36–37: The view of the Formal Garden from the Gothic Room in the main house.

LEFT: A view of the Formal Garden, looking north toward the Allée and Formal Greenhouse from Bunny's bedroom suite after a summer storm.

PAGES 40–41: The west side of the Formal Garden, looking south toward the main house. In the foreground, the Herb Garden and vegetable gardens surround the wishing well on the Lower Terrace. The Square Garden is in the center of the Middle Terrace, and toward the back is the fieldstone-paved Upper Terrace.

PAGES 42–43: A view of the axial path descending through the Middle and Lower Terraces to the Allée and on to the Formal Greenhouse.

PAGES 44–45: View of the canopy of the Allée and the axial path of the Formal Garden, looking south from the Schlumberger finial at the top of the Formal Greenhouse.

{ GARDENS IN VIRGINIA }

On the Upper Terrace, the path is laid in basket-weave- and herringbone-patterned brick. The Middle Terrace path is set in flagstone and bordered with clusters of lavender. The Lower Terrace path is paved in Rainbow Chip gravel mixed with a small amount of crushed oyster shells and bordered by two-foot-high cordon apple trees. A secondary three-foot-wide brick path rings the perimeter of the garden, and three-foot-wide paths of weathered stone cross the terraces from east to west.

On both sides of the axial path, the terraces are laid out in French-style parterres, each with a unique planting scheme. In the southwest corner of the Upper Terrace are the White Garden and the small Rose Garden. In spring, the White Garden blooms with Chinese wisteria, hosta, plantain lily, Japanese painted fern, lily of the valley, white globe allium, woodland phlox, white squill, witch hazel, and snake's head fritillary. The Rose Garden, a favorite grazing place for rabbits, is filled with white roses planted in a fifteen-square grid. Each rose bush is surrounded by clusters of pansies, and a low hedge of germander outlines each of the fifteen squares.

A hardy orange is the central focus on the east side of the Upper Terrace. Mrs. Mellon loved these trees, but her gardeners didn't. Their pointy thorns pierced the gardeners' hats when they were pruning the trees. One day, stonemason Harold Lovett asked her why she insisted on having so many hardy orange trees and told her that they had ruined his hat. Her response: "They are great trees for the birds to build their nests and to go and hide," and she offered to buy him a new hat.

More hardy oranges border the perimeter path, along with verbena and American boxwood, as well as fritillary, lady's mantle, *Epimedium*, and Virginia bluebell in the spring, and rosemary and lavender in the summer and fall. The Upper Terrace was originally planted with creeping bent grass, a favorite of Gerard Lambert. It is a luxurious grass that requires constant maintenance, and one Oak Spring gardener was assigned to it full-time. Lawn mowing was an exercise in the art of diplomacy. Permission had to be granted before any mowing took place. The housekeeper carried the verbal "request" to mow with the breakfast tray upstairs to the bedchamber. Even when

PAGES 46–47: The White Garden on the Upper Terrace in springtime.

PAGES 48–49: On the west side of the Upper Terrace, the fieldstone-covered area is to the left of the brick walkway, a holly tree is espaliered on the main house, the White Garden is in the upper right-hand corner, and the Rose Garden is to the right.

TOP LEFT: A seating area on the east side of the Upper Terrace.

BOTTOM LEFT: The gate on the west side of the Upper Terrace.

OPPOSITE: To make the colors of her flowers pop, Bunny contrasted them with gray foliage, such as the *Artemisia ludoviciana* 'Silver King' used here.

PAGES 52–53: The view from the Upper Terrace toward the schoolhouse in the northwest corner of the Formal Garden.

PAGE 54: Fleabane daisies and thyme grow through the cracks in the fieldstone on the Upper Terrace.

PAGE 55: The hardy orange tree on the east side of the Upper Terrace is underplanted with grape hyacinths and violets.

permission was granted, the mowing could not begin until 10:30 A.M., and all mowers had to be silenced by noon.

There was less mowing to be done by the 1970s, when the terrace grass was replaced with irregular pieces of fieldstone. The long, tedious process of building this stone terrace was entrusted to Tom Reed and Harold Lovett, stonemasons at the farm. The men quarried the stone from a field in nearby Warrenton and transported it to the farm, where they cut and shaped it by hand. They took special care to soften the sharp edges of the cut stones, giving each a worn, aged appearance. One day, while Tom was laying the stone, he caught Mrs. Mellon in her brimmed blue hat out of the corner of his eye. "Yoo hoo, young man," she called out to him. "You are laying that stone north to south and I want it to go east to west." So Tom began to pull up the stones and lay them east to west. With her knowing eye, Bunny patiently watched as the heavy pieces were lifted, shifted, and turned. When a corner of one of the stones cracked, Tom was about to

replace it, but Bunny stopped him, saying, "No, leave it just as it is—it gives character." Then she took out her own hammer, chipped off a few more corners, and sprinkled seeds of fleabane daisies and creeping thyme into the cracks. Today the wildflowers and herbs proliferate and the smoothed stone edges are barely visible.

Bunny's impeccable manners extended to her gardeners (she made them feel like they were family), and whenever she had guests she would conduct a round of introductions. As far as garden gear was concerned, she insisted on hats for everyone—herself included—for protection against the harsh rays of the sun. And she always kept an ample supply of cold drinks on hand. "When she told us to go and get a drink, we went and got a drink," recalls J. D. Tutwiler. "And if a supervisor questioned why we were taking a break, we told him that she told us to and that was the end of that!" Mr. and Mrs. Mellon—"They're why we're still here today," J. D. and Tommy concur.

The prominent features of the Middle Terrace are the Honey House, the Butterfly Garden, the Tea Garden, and the Square Garden. At the eastern end is the Honey House, a small, square cottage used for storing tools and supplies—not honey. Amid the gardening tools, bric-a-brac, and dried flowers hanging from the rafters is a step-in-fireplace suitable for open-hearth cooking and, displayed on a nearby wall, is Mrs. Mellon's 1987 Landscape Design Award from the American Horticultural Society. A clock on the front façade chimes the daytime hours. Right outside the Honey House is the Tea Garden, which is planted with Alpine strawberry, lemon balm, lemon verbena, ornamental allium, peppermint, spearmint (an important ingredient in the popular Rokeby Tea), sweet woodruff, and, in the spring, Triumph Tulip 'Shirley'.

ROKEBY TEA

4 Lipton tea bags
½ gallon water
2 lemons and 2 oranges, squeezed and strained
1 cup sugar
4–6 sprigs of mint

Add tea bags to ½ gallon of boiling water. Let steep six to eight minutes, remove tea bags, stir in sugar until dissolved, and stir in juice. Garnish with mint. Enjoy.

Next to the Honey House is the Butterfly Garden, a sometimes shady and cool locale with an advantageous view of the rest of the Formal Garden. It consists of a small square pool and two butterfly-shaped beds outlined with brick. (Butterflies symbolize the immortality of the human soul.) Snowdrops, the earliest of spring bulbs, flower in winter before the vernal equinox. Spring brings allium, columbine, *Artemisia* 'Silver Mound', forget-me-nots, pansies, and sedum. In early summer the beds are planted with catmint, columbine, creeping thyme, feverfew, floss flower, Japanese aster, *Lantana*, lavender, *Dianthus*, strawberries, sweet alyssum, and various herbs. The vibrant colors of the butterflies that are attracted to the plantings add a dimension of their own as they flutter through the lush beds. In winter, the beds' butterfly forms remain—a poignant memory of summer.

The Square Garden is an open lawn seeded with a sun-and-shade blend of bluegrass and perennial ryegrass in the middle of the Formal Garden. The open space brings balance to the overall garden design and offers rest to the eye. Crab apple trees punctuate the four corners. In summer, the surrounding border is filled with a wide variety of flowers, including bearded iris, catmint, columbine, Cuban oregano, lady's mantle, lamb's ear, lilies, pinks, sedum, Russian sage, speedwell, and wormwood. The paths around the Square Garden are lined with two-foot-high cordon apple varieties: Connell Red, Fireside,

Freedom, Golden Delicious, Haralred, Honeycrisp, and State Fair, all of which bear fruit in the fall.

One day a dandelion cropped up amid the cordon apple trees. Going about his daily chores, J. D. weeded the dandelion. It seemed like the right thing to do, as the entire staff had already been asked to dig up a field of unwanted dandelions. However, later that day Mrs. Mellon arrived in the garden with some friends in tow. "Where is my dandelion?" she asked J. D. "I want my friends to see it." When J. D. explained that he had weeded it, he was told, "Don't do it again." Mishaps like this led the gardeners to come up with a set of unofficial Oak Spring Garden rules:

{ GARDENS IN VIRGINIA }

Be very careful what you do.
Everything is a flower—until it's not.
Utilize anything and everything possible.
Go slow, take your time; no rushing.
When snipping, pinching, or pruning, follow the template
and keep it open so you can see the sky.

In summer, the paths around the Square Garden are aflutter with butterflies—the garden in flight. Fleabane daisies, purple and white petunias, Russian sage, *Artemisia* 'Silver Mound', *Verbena bonariensis*, and wood asters—a heavenly combination—are planted in groups of three, six, and nine along both sides of the paths. This scheme is a good example of a technique that Mrs. Mellon used to bring harmony to the garden. She selected plants in the tones, shades, and variations of light and shadow found in a single flower, a purple petunia, for instance, and then planted them in a triangular shape in multiples of three.

The Lower Terrace is a mix of lawn, vegetable gardens, and an Herb Garden. A Katherine crab apple was intentionally planted off center in a vegetable garden on the east side of the axial path. The base of the tree is circled by a garden bench, which in turn is ringed by Kingsville boxwoods. The rest of this garden is planted with roses and vegetables, including parsley, beets, and cabbages, sown in diagonal lines. Just to the west of the axial path is the Herb Garden. The aromas of basil, chervil, chives, leeks, oregano, and parsley waft over the garden's stepping-stone paths and nearby stone wishing well. Chipmunks hide in the cracks and crevices of the stone. At first J. D. plugged the openings, but he was instructed to unplug them so the chipmunks could get in and out freely.

The vegetable gardens on the west side of the axial path are planted with artichokes, broccoli, cabbages, cauliflower, field cress, kale, kohlrabi, lettuce, onions, spinach, and sorrel (for Mrs. Mellon's favorite sorrel soup). To the west of the vegetable gardens is a bed of red poppies and another of flax and marigold, in honor of Mr. Mellon's gray and yellow racing colors.

The six-foot-high stone wall surrounding the Formal Garden was whitewashed to keep it from looking too "stonified." Changing patterns of light and shadow play

PAGES 70–71: The Katherine crab apple tree on the east side of the Lower Terrace in full bloom.

OPPOSITE: Kingsville boxwoods encircle the crab apple tree.

TOP RIGHT: The Herb Garden on the west side of the Lower Terrace.

BOTTOM RIGHT: A flourishing dill plant.

PAGE 74 LEFT, FROM TOP TO BOTTOM: The vegetable gardens, looking north, west, and east.

PAGES 74–75: A Darlington Oak towers above the east side of the Lower Terrace.

PAGES 76–77: Tulips and pansies in springtime.

PAGES 78–79: The South Vegetable Garden and wishing well on a mid-June morning.

PAGES 80-81: The South and North Vegetable Gardens and the Herb Garden at the height of summer.

PAGES 82–83: The East Vegetable Garden on the Lower Terrace.

PAGE 83 TOP AND BOTTOM: Kale and summer squash in one of the vegetable gardens.

{ GARDENS IN VIRGINIA }

PAGES 84–85: View of the pool and Lower Terrace from the Basket House.

PAGE 85 TOP AND BOTTOM RIGHT: The flower and vegetable beds near the Basket House pool. Bunny dipped the baskets in the pool to refresh the fibers.

OPPOSITE and RIGHT: An assortment of the baskets on display in the Basket House.

PAGES 88–89: The Lower Terrace, abloom with columbine, azaleas, tulips, fleabane daisies, and allium in spring.

PAGES 90–91: The flower beds by the Basket House pool and schoolhouse.

PAGE 92: The schoolhouse steps.

PAGE 93: A view of the east and west flower beds along the north wall.

on the stone throughout the day as the sun moves across the sky. Hinged to the wall at the point where the axial path meets the Allée are two handcrafted wooden gates in the French medieval style, complete with hand-forged latches. Bay trees flank the gates. There is an open-door policy during the day, but at night the gates are closed. In Mrs. Mellon's day, whimsical cast-metal finials designed by Jane Sage Canfield topped the two gateposts: a ground-hog-shaped one on the east post and a rabbit-shaped one on the west post.

Apple trees (Fireside, Snow Sweet, and State Fair) are espaliered in a candelabra form on the east side of the south-facing wall. In Bunny's day, the palette of the flower beds in front of this part of the wall was primarily dark with pops of color: sunflowers, cosmos, zinnias, and other orange and dark-colored flowers. Sweet Sixteen, State Fair, and Honeycrisp apples are espaliered on the west side of the wall. Here, the flower beds had a lighter palette. In the spring, purple pansies and violets stole the show, replaced in summer by soft gray lamb's ear, this-tle, foxtail lily, lady's mantle, and golden sunflowers. In autumn, common mulleins, their seeds having been spread by the wind, stand tall like sentries atop the stone wall. A six-foot-wide gravel path, edged with Kingsville box-woods, runs east to west along the beds. A foster holly anchors one end and a crab apple the other.

Water features at the edges of the garden are not for irrigation purposes but for atmosphere; the soothing sound of the moving water creates a sense of calm and peace. On the west side, a narrow pool fronts the Basket House, which is reached by a sliver of a bridge over the pool. Symmetrical beds bordering the pool are filled with daisies, foxtail lily, phlox, sedum, thistle, and wallflowers. The bottom of the pool is painted blue to reflect the sky. To generate a lovely, gentle trickling sound, a floating wall is inset in the pool just low enough for the water to spill over it. For visual appeal, jets beneath the water's surface create a rippling effect.

On the east side of the garden, water is piped from beneath the Honey House to a spout at the side of the main house, where it trickles into a small stone basin. From there it flows along a trough to the back of the gar-

{ GARDENS IN VIRGINIA }

PAGE 94 TOP: Bunny pruning a holly tree espaliered on the south wall.

PAGES 94 BOTTOM AND 95: Two varieties of three-tier espalier forms.

LEFT, ABOVE, AND BELOW: The flower beds along the north wall in different seasons.

PAGE 98: Details of the flowers and fruit trees planted along the north wall, including poppies, globe thistle, tulips, irises, *Rudbeckia*, petunias, and pears.

PAGE 99: Water spilling from a spout near the Honey House into the water trough that runs along the eastern side of the garden.

PAGES 100–1: A crepe myrtle in the northeast corner of the Croquet Lawn in spring.

PAGE 102 TOP: The crepe myrtle in winter.

PAGE 102 BOTTOM: A crab apple tree at the northern end of the Croquet Lawn. The roof of the wedding cake gazebo is at the lower right.

PAGES 102–3: The west side of the Formal Garden under a blanket of snow.

den, where it turns and splashes into another stone basin. Bunny wanted a little waterfall there, and she needed a certain kind of rock for the water to flow over. Tommy Reed found the perfect one—a smooth stone shaped like a turtle shell. It is still there today. At this point, the water recycles back to the Honey House. A group of chairs is set up near the stone basin for the comfort and benefit of the listener.

A Colonial-style bowling green—a rectangular-shaped lawn used for playing croquet and other lawn games—runs parallel to the trough. In earlier days, a hornbeam hedge extended along its periphery. Today a star magnolia fills the corner bed; beneath it are fritillaries and other shade-loving plants, including astilbe, *Epimedium*, and *Meconopsis*, with its distinctive, poppy-like blue flowers.

The Allée is a 127-foot-long walkway flanked by pleached Mary Potter crab apple trees (thirty on each side). A metal framework, built by Everett Hicks, an expert arborist who worked with Mrs. Mellon for many years, arches over the walkway. The trees' branches have been trained over the curve of the framework in a crisscross pattern, creating a leafy canopy that on sunny days casts a lattice-like shadow along the length of the path. The Allée has become the landmark feature of Oak Spring. The crab apples were planted in the late 1950s as saplings, about 10 feet tall, with a caliper (the diameter of the trunk at 12 inches above the ground) of about 1½ inches. Today the caliper of the largest tree is about 5½ inches, and the trees fully cover the frame. Since the initial planting, only two of the trees have been replaced. The Allée's trees are regularly pruned from January through March, as are all the other fruit trees on the property. Pruning must be done after a hard freeze to prevent the trees from weakening. There is a second, and sometimes even a third, round of light pruning in mid-summer. The Allée's frame collapsed in the mid-1980s under the weight of an early snow. Usually, when a heavy snowfall is forecast, the frame is propped up by two-by-fours. But this

{ GARDENS IN VIRGINIA }

one early snow took everyone by surprise. It required the skill of two metalsmiths to replace the entire frame.

Though a showstopper throughout the year, the Allée is at its most enchanting in spring, when the crab apples' pink-tinged white flowers burst into bloom. And when the wind whips up a flurry of petals, everyone at Oak Spring calls it "snow in spring."

Two flower beds, each 4½ feet wide, border the Allée. The beds are rimmed with Kingsville boxwoods and filled with flowers of the season. In spring there are tulips, pansies, fritillaries, and *Muscari* in shades of purple, pink, white, and yellow. Summer brings dusty miller, white impatiens, coleus, heliotrope, feverfew, and *Caladium*. In fall the beds are filled with chrysanthemums, and the color of the crab apple fruit is a deep crimson.

The Allée leads to the Formal Greenhouse, the culmination of the central axial path. Completed in 1960, this Lord & Burnham "aluminum classic" is a symmetrical

{ GARDENS IN VIRGINIA }

{ GARDENS IN VIRGINIA }

structure, with two long glass greenhouses extending from a central pavilion. The steep pitch of the greenhouses' roofs is the most favorable angle for the sun to strike the glass. Their brick-lined floors are sunken into the ground for greater insulation. Citrus trees are espaliered along the back walls, and potting trays running the length of each greenhouse are filled with topiaries, seedlings, and tender annuals and perennials. Two shallow pools front the greenhouses, creating a moat-like effect. To the east of the pools stands the so-called wedding cake gazebo. This lattice-walled structure was built to display the cake at the wedding of Bunny's daughter, Eliza Lloyd, on May 15, 1968. It has served as a poolside seating area ever since.

From September through May, the Formal Greenhouse was Bunny's winter paradise. She cultivated green flowers (green zinnia 'Envy', *Nicotiana alata* 'Lime Green', and lady's mantle), alternately referred to as "witches" and "mysteries," in the greenhouse, using them to great effect in bouquets and flower beds to "deepen, brighten and add subtlety" to other plantings.

Also cultivated in the greenhouse were little herb trees. Bunny described them in "Green Flowers and Herb Trees," an article she wrote for the December 1965 issue of *Vogue*: "Years ago I experimented with growing rosemary, thyme, myrtle and santolina into small standards in the shape of bay trees, varying from ten inches to three feet in height. . . . The original clipping for the myrtle trees came from Mt. Vernon, where Mr. Robert B. Fisher, the head gardener, is generous and carries on the exchange of plants as once George Washington did." It took two years to shape an herb tree to her satisfaction, and as the trees matured, she shared them with family and friends. "A pinched leaf of rosemary, thyme, or santolina will bring the scent of a country garden into any room," she wrote. "Some friends who cook keep their trees in the kitchen where the trimming of a tree becomes the flavor of the stew."

Cuttings from plants in the garden were also propagated in the greenhouse: dwarf *Artemisia*, dwarf sage, *Geranium* 'Johnson's Blue', lavender, *Plumbago*, white strawberries, santolina, cyclamen, *Gerbera*, and primrose. In 1959 she and her gardener Charles M. Pecora were awarded first prize blue ribbon for a cyclamen in class no.

{ GARDENS IN VIRGINIA }

PAGES 120–21: In the Formal Greenhouse, Bunny's tradition of cultivating and pruning topiaries continues to this day.

LEFT: Bunny's watercolor of a flowering cyclamen.

OPPOSITE: A potted Mixed Hardy cyclamen in the production greenhouse.

PAGES 124–25: Trompe l'oeil murals by artist Fernand Renard entirely cover the central pavilion in the Formal Greenhouse .

PAGES 126–27: Details of the trompe l'oeil murals. Painted doors open to reveal a storage cupboard and potting counter.

646 at the International Flower Show in New York, and the next year she and Mr. Pecora were awarded first prize for a cyclamen in class no. 642. She also earned a Cultural Certificate for *Cyclamen* 'Pride of Zehlendorf' at the Winter Garden Show, sponsored by the Horticultural Society of New York on February 18, 1959.

In the Formal Greenhouse's central pavilion, floor-to-ceiling doors conceal valuable storage space and serve double duty as canvases for trompe l'oeil murals featuring a few of Mrs. Mellon's favorite things: sapphire wedding bands (plus an actual hook to safeguard the real ones while she was gardening), pruning shears, a favorite denim hat, a drawing of the Formal Greenhouse, a red geranium, the French flag, gourds, baskets, and, hidden inside a cabinet door, a garden smock. The artist Fernand Renard began this work in France and completed it at Oak Spring in 1960.

Atop the pavilion is a decorative finial in the shape of an urn filled with a bouquet of rose hips, lilies, daisies, tulips, thistles, and artichoke foliage. Designed by Jean Schlumberger, the French jewelry designer, and executed in lead by Robert Bradford, it is the crowning touch to the classic greenhouse architecture and brims with symbolism.

The artwork displayed at Oak Spring reveals Bunny's devotion to the Dutch masters, including Jan Baptist van Fornenburgh (1585–ca. 1649), Johannes van Bronkhorst (1648–1726), and Pieter van Loo (1731–1784), all renowned for their realistic botanical paintings. The finial is crafted in much the same tradition. Its flowers represent different seasons (rose hips—fall; lilies and tulips—spring; daisies—summer). Some are depicted as wilted, past the height of their bloom, and one lone stem is intentionally fastened to the roof, signifying the ephemerality of life so touchingly captured in Psalm 103: 15–16, as Mrs. Mellon noted in her catalogue *Flora*: "As for man, his days are as grass: as a flower of the field, so he flourisheth. For the wind passeth over it, and it is gone."

LEFT: One of Jean Schlumberger's sketches of the finial for the top of the Formal Greenhouse.

OPPOSITE: Schlumberger's elaborate bouquet was executed in lead by Robert Bradford.

PAGES 130–31: Apple trees along Peach Tree Lane in autumn.

PAGE 132, CLOCKWISE FROM TOP: A grove of hardy orange trees; Golden Delicious apples ripening; Arkansas Black apples ready for harvest; Asian pears at the front of the main house.

PAGE 133, CLOCKWISE FROM TOP LEFT: Orchard baskets full of Winesap apples; an abundant cluster of crab apples; Red Delicious apples ready for the kitchen; apples being pressed into cider; Randy Embrey, the head gardener, harvesting apples.

PAGE 134: An apple tree weathers a winter storm.

PAGE 135: The Apple House at dawn.

PAGES 136–37: Bunny's daughter, Eliza's skating pond in autumn.

{ GARDENS IN VIRGINIA }

{ GARDENS IN VIRGINIA }

OAK SPRING FARM

According to Randy Embrey, Oak Spring's head gardener, "Orchards of fruit trees are nestled in clusters throughout the farm and provide a year-round supply of some of the tastiest Pomona grown in the State of Virginia." Some varieties date back to the days of Thomas Jefferson: Hewes Crab (cider-making), Spitzenburg and Newtown Pippin (dessert), and the ever-popular Greengage plum (considered one of the finest varieties of plums). Other vintage varieties cultivated today include: apples—Baldwin, Cortland, Golden Russet, Snow Apple, Tolman, and Yellow Newton Pippin; peaches—Loring, Redhaven, and Reliance; pears—Anjou, Kieffer, Max Red Bartlett, Moonglow, and Summercrisp; and plums—Shiro.

The fruit trees *are* the sculptures at Oak Spring and are given careful, systematic attention. Pruning is an art form and one of the more prominent manifestations of Mrs. Mellon's philosophy and aesthetic. The goal is to open up the tree to let in light and air, and provide circulation, enabling rainwater to reach the beds and roots below. Most of the tree trimming takes place in winter in a manner reminiscent of historical French pruning methods. Each tree is trimmed from the top down. The bare branches are cut back to the second or third node of the past season's growth. All dead wood, crossing branches, and spindly side shoots are removed. This skill is gardener specific, and a trained eye can spot which gardener pruned which tree.

Mrs. Mellon wanted to keep everything on the property looking natural. As J. D. Tutwiler recalls, "In the fall, when it was time to mow, we would pick up the old apples that had fallen to the ground and push the good ones towards the tree trunk, mow, and then spread the good apples back below the tree again, as if they'd just fallen." It was part of the autumn ritual.

In 1987 a new Apple House was built to process the apples. A twenty-foot-long conveyor belt moves the apples through washing and drying stages, readying them for storage in atmosphere-controlled lockers, assuring a ready supply of apples year round.

The farm is divided by Rokeby Road. The property to the west of the road is called Rokeby Farm, and the

property to the east is called Oak Spring Farm. To support Mr. Mellon's fox-hunting and horse-breeding operations, there were six barns for the hunters, mares, and yearlings, as well as a pony barn that was the exclusive domain of Bunny's daughter, Eliza Lloyd, who staged theatrical productions there. The broodmare barn was constructed on the Oak Spring side in the 1950s and has recently been converted into housing for visiting scholars by the Oak Spring Garden Foundation.

The paddocks and fields near the main house were reserved for the horses, so the Mellons could watch them from the house or when they went out for a walk. In his autobiography, *Reflections in a Silver Spoon*, written with his friend John Baskett, Paul Mellon recalled how much he enjoyed "the sight of mares and foals grazing in green fields, or yearlings running wild and throwing themselves about, even though it puts your heart in your mouth."

Also on the Oak Spring side, near the parking area for the main house, is a small gazebo that looks like a bird-house. Encircled with plantings of feverfew and poppies, it is draped in morning glories in the summer and fall. Nearby is a small pet cemetery.

After Mrs. Mellon's death, a new production greenhouse and garden were built on the Oak Spring side. The flowers used to create floral arrangements for the main house and for Oak Spring Garden Foundation events are grown there, as are plants for the Formal Greenhouse and Formal Garden.

More than 4,000 head of cattle—Angus, Herefords, Shorthorns, and Charolais—used to graze in the pastures on both the Oak Spring and Rokeby sides. Mr. Mellon maximized the field potential through routine cattle rotation.

Many of Mrs. Mellon's little herb trees, flowers, and plants were nurtured in a complex of production greenhouses dating back to the 1930s. They are located on the Rokeby side. There is also a spacious room for potting plants and flower arranging, as well as a lath house where citrus trees are kept in summer to shade them from the sun.

On a dismal, rainy day in April 1969, members of the American Herb Society were invited to Oak Spring for lunch and a tour of the garden. Paul Mellon brightened the gloomy atmosphere with a poem he wrote in honor of the occasion:

A WELCOME TO OAK SPRING

Pleased as I am to welcome you—
My thumb was never green, it's true,
And horticultural knack and lore
Will pass me by, forevermore.
My country seat is on a horse,
And though I love the land, of course,
I have a horse's point of view,
And like a horse I favor too,
Clover and bluegrass deeply growing,
Green of spring and summer's mowing.
But Bunny has a magic touch,
And well we know, there isn't much

Of anything on earth that grows
From mighty oak to tiny rose
Eludes her touch. From bloom to root, her
Heart is a gardening computer,
While in her head, there's a whole college
Comprising horticultural knowledge.
Now she will lead you on a tour
Of fragrant bowers (and fine manure),
Through gardens gay with blooms and shrubs
And tender shoots in pots and tubs,
Through palaces of crystal glass
With tropic fruits and flowers, en masse,
Through scents and sights in bright profusion
(Through Latin names, to my confusion!)
Now it's my very happy duty
To urge you toward these scenes of beauty,
And should some beast obscure your view,
Forgive us—we grow horses too!

LEFT: Down the hill from the main house is the springhouse, where cool, clear water flows into a ravine.

ABOVE: Morning glories climb up a gazebo by the pet cemetery.

PAGES 140–41: Mist rises on a pond near the pony barn.

PAGE 141 RIGHT, FROM TOP TO BOTTOM: The weather vane crowning the pony barn; a crab apple tree in bloom nearby; view of the Bull Run Mountains in the distance.

PAGES 142–43: The pond by the pony barn, covered in snow.

{ GARDENS IN VIRGINIA }

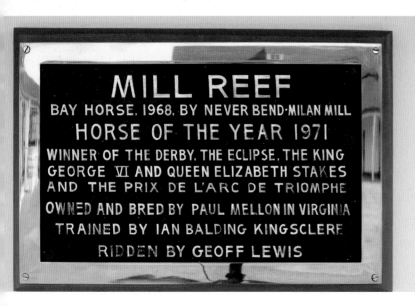

MILL REEF
BAY HORSE, 1968. BY NEVER BEND-MILAN MILL
HORSE OF THE YEAR 1971
WINNER OF THE DERBY, THE ECLIPSE, THE KING
GEORGE VI AND QUEEN ELIZABETH STAKES
AND THE PRIX DE L'ARC DE TRIOMPHE
OWNED AND BRED BY PAUL MELLON IN VIRGINIA
TRAINED BY IAN BALDING KINGSCLERE
RIDDEN BY GEOFF LEWIS

{ GARDENS IN VIRGINIA }

Page 144 left, from top to bottom: Horse stalls converted into guest rooms surround the courtyard of the broodmare barn; a painting of Paul Mellon's famous horse Mill Reef; a memorial plaque.

Pages 144–45: The broodmare barn is located in an open field.

Pages 146–47: A wildflower meadow in the vegetable garden on the farm.

Left: Zucchini growing near a pasture.

Above: Zinnias are among the flowers cultivated in the farm's cutting garden.

Below: Nasturtiums hug a pasture fence.

Pages 150–51: The pond near the pony barn in spring.

Page 151 Right: A crop of sunflowers reaches toward the sky.

Pages 152–53: Sunrise on the farm.

The funeral prayer card that Mrs. Mellon chose for herself before her death featured a photograph of a sunflower on the front and Psalm 23 on the back. Much of the psalm's imagery—green pastures, still waters, paths of righteousness, prepared table—evokes Oak Spring, where one sees "the miraculous in the common." She wanted nothing in her soft, gentle, and lovely garden to be obvious, so that when you went away, you would remember only the peace. Yes, only the peace.

OAK SPRING GARDEN LIBRARY

"This library, which includes manuscripts going back to the 1300s amounts to a working collection for it is in continuous use. From it I learned much about pruning, growing, and designing, for past methods were often ahead of ours."

—Bunny Mellon, "Green Flowers and Herb Trees,"
Vogue, December 1965

The Oak Spring Garden Library is Mrs. Mellon's horticultural legacy. Containing more than sixteen thousand rare books, manuscripts, and works of art dating back to the fourteenth century—all collected over her lifetime—it is a working library for scholars and students alike.

The library, a gift from Mr. Mellon, blends seamlessly into the rolling landscape northwest of the house and garden. The rectangular, whitewashed-stone contemporary building was designed by Edward Larrabee Barnes and completed in 1981. A new wing designed by local architect Thomas Beach was added in 1997 to accommodate the ever-growing collection.

The front door is reached across a terrace where "wildflowers grow where they will"—a self-sown wildflower garden in summer. A large-scale horizontal sundial over the entrance tracks the movement of the sun and tells the time of day. Nearby are a hardy orange tree and a variety of apple trees—Albemarle Pippin, Gala, Golden Delicious, McIntosh, and Winesap—an ideal setting for a garden library.

The first room one encounters is a long, narrow study area in the new wing with a soaring, double-height ceiling. A circular stairs leads to a balcony that overlooks the study area. Mrs. Mellon's well-worn sidesaddle is on display in one corner. In the center of the room is a long study table, and bookcases line the walls. One of Mrs. Mellon's treasures is stored in this room—the oversize, green-striped scrapbook that Jackie Kennedy made for her as a thank-you for designing the Rose Garden for President Kennedy. It traces the history of the garden and is filled with pressed flowers, some of the first sketches Mrs. Mellon

PAGES 154–55: The north façade of the Oak Spring Garden Library.

ABOVE: The balcony in the new wing of the library, overlooking the study area.

LEFT: The spiral staircase leading to the balcony in the new wing.

OPPOSITE TOP: Bunny perusing a book in the library's main room.

OPPOSITE BOTTOM: The main room in the original building.

PAGE 158: Bunny's study table, overlooked by a reproduction of one of her prized Rothkos (the original was sold at auction).

PAGE 159 LEFT AND RIGHT: Two paintings of medicinal plants that Bunny and Hubert de Givenchy found in France's Loire Valley: *Fritillaria pallidiflora* (LEFT) and *Mandragora Officinarum* (RIGHT).

PAGE 160, FROM TOP TO BOTTOM: A miniature greenhouse that was a gift from Hubert de Givenchy; *Hortus Eystettensis* by Basilius Besler, 1613; a page on pruning in Jean-Baptiste de La Quintinie's *The Compleat Gard'ner*, 1693, and a key to the King's Gate at the Potager du Roi.

PAGE 161: *An Oak Spring Herbaria*, 2009, one of the catalogues of the library's collection that Bunny began publishing in 1989.

PAGE 162: A French library ladder; Flemish, English, and German paintings; and a table crafted at Oak Spring to display Basilius Besler's *Hortus Eystettensis* form a tableau next to the Rothko.

PAGE 163: An early eighteenth-century lacca povera bureau. Its decoupage ornamentation is engraved and hand colored.

made of the garden, family photographs, and humorous comments. On display in an adjacent gallery are her cherished twentieth-century photograph of the gardeners at the Potager du Roi in Versailles; a group of eight French paintings, each illustrating a different medicinal plant—Aloe, *Carlina acaulis*, *Datura metel*, *Fritillaria pallidiflora*, *Lavandula stoechas*, *Mandragora officinarum*, *Ruscus hypoglossum*, and *Veratrum album*; and two paintings by the early seventeenth-century Italian artist Girolamo Pini, a study of flowers with an iris in the center, ca. 1614, and a study of flowers with a fritillary in the center, ca. 1614.

A narrow stair leads to the second story and Mrs. Mellon's storybook-tower workroom. It is a small room with panoramic views of the farm and the mountains beyond. There is a tiny fireplace in one corner, a treasure trove of working drawings and garden plans stored in an upright roll file in another, a desk, and a chair. A country hutch painted blue holds personal treasures, including a small Renoir still life of plums.

In the original building, the eighty-foot-long, double-height main room has a pair of floor-to-ceiling windows in one of the long walls. Bookcases line the facing wall, and rolling ladders access the top shelves. Bookcases also line the balcony that overlooks the room. On sunny days it is flooded with light, and by early afternoon the librarians begin their daily ritual of shuttering the windows to protect the precious manuscripts, paintings, and artifacts. The furniture in the center of the space is arranged like a comfortable living room and includes two linen sofas and several side chairs slipcovered in prints and checks. This

seating area has a sweeping view of the country landscape through the large picture windows. Foot-long logs of seasoned apple wood crackle on chilly mornings in the fireplace. The fireplace's stone surround was transported in two pieces from a house in England and installed by Tom Reed and Harold Lovett.

On the same wall as the large windows hangs a reproduction of one of Mrs. Mellon's prized paintings by Mark Rothko (the original was sold at auction). Tom Reed laid the stone for the "Rothko wall." The three-foot-thick wall was almost completed when it was decided that it "just isn't right. Move it out." The wall was demolished and the masons had to begin again. It took a week to complete, and in the end it was perfect.

Books shaped and informed Bunny's pursuits in the garden. They helped her blend past practices with those of the present. Her "Pentateuch" consisted of *The Compleat Gard'ner; or, Directions for Cultivating and Right Ordering of Fruit-Gardens and Kitchen-Gardens* by Jean-Baptiste de La Quintinie, 1693; *Phytographia curiosa* by Abraham Munting, 1713; *The Flower-Garden Display'd, In Above Four Hundred Curious Representations of the Most Beautiful Flowers* by Robert Furber, 1734; *Le Jardin Fruitier* by Louis Claude Noisette, 1821; and *Flower Guide, Revised and With New Illustrations: Wild Flowers East of the Rockies* by Chester Albert Reed, 1920.

In 1989 Mrs. Mellon began to publish a series of catalogues of the library's holdings in an effort to make the collection available to gardeners, scholars, and researchers. The first, *An Oak Spring Sylva* (1989), showcases forty-six books on trees and shrubs; *An Oak Spring Pomona* (1990) features one hundred books, manuscripts, drawings, and paintings on fruit trees; *An Oak Spring Flora* (1997) consists of one hundred items on flowers; and *An Oak Spring Herbaria* (2009) is an extensive study on herbs and herbalists beginning with the late Middle Ages.

The torch has been passed to the Oak Spring Garden Foundation, which is continuing Mrs. Mellon's tradition of supporting and encouraging the study of horticulture and garden design. The enduring beauty of the Oak Spring Garden is a glorious testament to the library at work.

TRINITY EPISCOPAL CHURCH

At Christmastime, the scent of the southern favorite *Buxus*, or "boxwood" as it is commonly called, wafts over the grounds of Trinity Episcopal Church in the village of Upperville. The sandstone buildings that make up this Meade Parish complex surround a circular courtyard paved with cobblestones in a scallop-shell pattern. At the center of the courtyard stands a sheltering hackberry tree. The buildings were gifts to the parish from Paul and Rachel Mellon. Cox Parish Hall is to the north, Piedmont Children's Center, sited just across John S. Mosby Highway, is to the south, the rectory (now the church office) is to the west, and the church itself is to the east. It is the third church building to stand on this site. The first, built in 1842, "was taken down because of extreme dampness," according to the church's website. The second was completed in 1895. The third was begun in 1951, and the first service was held on September 25, 1960. In his opening remarks, the parish rector, the Reverend Robert Cox, said, "The first words to be said from this pulpit must be words of thanksgiving—thanks to God for His inspiration of beauty, and thanks to those who have made that inspiration a reality, here, in this place."

As recorded in Trinity's archives, Paul Mellon contributed financially to the church on May 4, 1941, and became a vestryman in December 1946. By the time the Mellons married in 1948, Bunny had become an active member in the Mary Neville Guild, the fund-raising arm of the church. She also created floral arrangements for the altar. At a guild meeting in 1948, the treasurer announced that there was a surplus of $300, and, as guild member Mary Lee de Butts wrote in *A History of the Mary D. Neville Guild*, a "fierce argument ensued as to whether to spend it on painting the inside walls of the church, badly smoked by the coal furnace, or to buy cushions to make the hard wooden pews more suitable." Bunny attended that meeting, and, according to de Butts, when the debate ended, she said "in her quiet way that she hoped we wouldn't change anything in the building until she had an opportunity to talk with Paul about it, that he was interested in the church and would like to do something for Upperville."

As Bunny well knew, the truth was that the old building lacked a proper foundation and was riddled with termites. The vestry had plans for a new building—one with a red brick exterior. Katherine Grayson Wilkins and Cabell Grayson of Upperville remember their father and uncle, both vestrymen, telling them of the vestry's meeting with Paul Mellon to ask for a contribution toward a new building. Their request for money was initially met with silence, and then Mr. Mellon made a proposal, "If we pay for the new building, can we change the design?"

Bunny later recorded her recollection of her husband's discussion with her about a new church building. "There is a resolution if you are willing and interested to go to work—I can help you. I can help out financially, but my calendar and obligations are so full already that it would be impossible for me to add another large commitment. This will be hard work. You will experience, most of all, the mixed thoughts and emotions of members of the Parish where you have just become a new member."

Bunny wrote in her journal that she couldn't sleep that night; her mind was racing with new ideas and childhood memories. "Living in France at a young age I was drawn to the small stone churches in villages surrounded by wheat fields, flax and forests. The doors were always unlocked. The spirit inside spoke of years of comforting quiet and peace. Many stones had the single word 'Merci' engraved to commemorate a loved one. In summer, small bouquets of wildflowers lay near the altar and often there would be a silent figure bowed in prayer on his return home from the fields and vineyards." The churches she had admired were small but they were "landmarks in rural communities"—communities like Upperville. The next morning she told Paul, "I'll try—I have a good idea how to begin." And she plunged in. Mr. Mellon recalled her enthusiasm for her building projects in his autobiography, *Reflections in a Silver Spoon*. The "beautiful church in Upperville" was on his list of her accomplishments.

H. Page Cross, a personal friend of the Mellons, signed on as architect. W. J. Hanback, a highly respected local builder in nearby Warrenton, served as general contractor, and Robert Hanback was the on-site foreman. Mrs. Mellon also reached out to Perry Wheeler, a prominent Washington, D.C., landscape architect, and Charlotte Noland, the remarkable woman who was the founder of her alma mater, Foxcroft School, in Middleburg, Virginia.

Perry Wheeler and Mrs. Mellon met in the late 1950s and developed a strong friendship. He was a kindred spirit when it came to designing gardens, sharing a keen sense of what was "right and appropriate," as Bunny's friend Deeda Blair observed. "Together they created wonderful gardens." The two collaborators had many late night phone conversations, working out their ideas and making plans for their many projects.

In her journal, Mrs. Mellon expressed deep admiration for Charlotte Noland, who had "taught us the importance of fairness, truth, kindness, and courage that among many simple ways, defined enjoyment in life. I turned to her for advice and help in building the church in Upperville. Miss Charlotte was a true Virginian and proud of the idea that the history of the past could inspire people of the future."

The first two churches had been oriented north–south, but the orientation of the new building was changed to east–west, so that the altar would be positioned at the eastern end, in keeping with time-honored tradition. Mrs. Mellon wrote, "The church is not a Norman church as it has often been described. We incorporated ideas and designs from many different sources." Indeed, Cross, who had studied at the École des Beaux-Arts in Paris, adapted various elements of twelfth- and thirteenth-century French country church architecture, including a modified cruciform plan with shallow transepts and Gothic arches.

The parish hall was built in 1950 for community events and to serve as the church meeting place while the old church was being torn down and the new one built. The cornerstone of the new church is dated 1955–1960, although it took much longer to build. "I've been on this project twelve years," parishioner and church historian Gray Coyner remembers Mrs. Mellon saying.

Constructed entirely by local craftsmen "under the direction of Robert Hanback," as George H. Glaysher writes in *Trinity Episcopal Church*, the church was built of native sandstone quarried in nearby Warrenton and hand-cut by Robert Hanback. Stone from the original 1842 church was incorporated into the second church and again into the third. "With the exception of artists who have contributed particular details, men of the countryside who have been trained in the arts of stone cutting, masonry and carpentry, are responsible for the entire construction," Mrs. Mellon jotted down in her notes. In honor of medieval building traditions, blacksmiths even forged the chisels that the masons used on the project. These men were a patient lot. The cobblestone for the courtyard was sourced in North Carolina by Perry Wheeler, and it was redone several times until the scallop-shell pattern was perfect; one wonders how many other things were done and redone. Upon completion of the church, the Mellons presented medallions to each of the craftsmen in appreciation of and gratitude for their work.

Bunny described the spiritual impact of the church's design in her journal, "The church was designed to show reverence for God, the wildflowers and plants carved on the pews, the beehives and fish, the animals and squirrels in the stone columns. The sun shines through the windows casting shadows on the stones, and the wooden cross was inspired by one in Chartres Cathedral."

The entrance to the church is through double wooden doors in the bell tower. The doors look as old as the ones Martin Luther made so famous and are operated with hand-forged hinges and pulls in the shape of horse heads, a subtle allusion to Upperville's location in the heart of Virginia Hunt Country. A clock adorns the tower façade, and Westminster bells ring hourly every day from nine o'clock in the morning until six o'clock in the evening. An inscription on the great bell reads: "These bells are dedicated to the men of this countryside who, by the skill of their hands, have built this church."

In the vestibule, the center beam is intentionally set slightly off-center to suggest the imperfection of man. The center aisle of the nave, laid with custom-designed cobblestone pavers like an axial path in a garden, is bordered on each side by narrow oak pews. The ends of the pews were hand-carved by Heinz Warneke with botanical motifs representing all the seasons: oak, holly, barley columbine, rose, ivy, fern, grape, trillium, pear, cherry, thistle, dogwood, and lily. The seats are padded with thick blue velvet cushions. The oak tree, associated with strength and long life, is depicted in the imagery, and its wood was used for the ceiling beams, pews, and the pulpit.

The soaring ceiling is painted blue. The struts supporting the rafters form triangles, the symbol of the Holy Trinity. American, State of Virginia, and ecclesiastical flags hang from the base of the ceiling along the side walls.

There are six stained-glass arched windows in the nave, three on each side, depicting biblical stories in the tradition of *Biblia pauperum*, or visual scripture for the poor or illiterate. The windows were designed and made by Joep Nicolas in his studio in Venlo, Netherlands, in 1959. According to the artist's daughter, Sylvia Nicolas, "The glass for these windows was probably manufac-

tured in England or Germany using a mouth-blown, 'new antique' method." On the north side there are scenes from the Old Testament, New Testament, and Apocrypha, including the Creation, symbolized by the image of God surrounded by the sun, the moon, and the stars; the patriarchs Noah, Abraham, Isaac, and Jacob; Saints Joachim and Anne, whose story is told in the Apocrypha; the Annunciation; and the Visitation. The relatively dim northern light represents the unenlightened world before the birth of Christ.

The windows on the south side, filled with natural light in the daytime, depict Christ as the light of the world, beginning with the Visitation of the Magi at Christ's birth, the Last Supper, and Pentecost, and ending with the figures of the four evangelists, Matthew, Mark, Luke, and John, and the missionaries Saint Peter and Saint Paul. The windows were commissioned by Paul Mellon and given in memory of Mary Conover Brown Mellon, his first wife and the mother of his two children. Dieter Goldkuhle, the Washington National Cathedral's principal stained-glass-window fabricator, installed the windows.

In the north transept hangs a large memorial plaque dedicated to Charlotte Noland. It reads: "This children's corner is given in honor of Charlotte Haxall Noland Founder of Foxcroft School in Recognition of her great Love and Understanding of Youth A.D. 1962."

In the south transept, on the east-facing wall, is the dedication window, a circular stained-glass window featuring an oak tree in blues and greens surrounded by an inscription: "This Church is Given to the Glory of God by Rachel and Paul Mellon. And of Thine own have we Given Thee." The inscription appears to have no beginning and no end—a symbol of God's love. It is one of three windows created for the church by Rowan LeCompte, who crafted more than forty windows in the Washington National Cathedral. The second is well hidden and the third is now in the Cameron Art Museum in Wilmington, North Carolina. A pair of stained-glass windows set in the south wall of the south transept is original to the second church building. Dedicated to the Mann family and dated 1880–1919, each depicts a figure holding an open Bible.

Warneke designed and crafted the hexagonal oak pulpit located at the south transept. The six sides, representing the days of creation, are carved with grapes and vines, symbols of the blood of Christ and the relationship between God and His people. On five of the edges between the six panels Warneke carved figures of John Chrysostom, Martin Luther, John Donne, Jonathan Edwards, and Phillips Brooks. The wrought-iron lectern, crafted by the metalwork firm P. A. Fiebiger, can be adjusted up and down, depending on the height of the speaker.

Meaningful imagery is also carved into the limestone imposts above the piers of the arches leading to the transepts. The images include a "Pelican in Her Piety"; a Ram with his Herd; an ichthus, an acrostic for "Jesus Christ, Son of God, Savior," in the shape of a fish—a secret code for early believers; a Unicorn (probably Mrs. Mellon's favorite); and a Phoenix, a symbol of the Resurrection. It is believed that Heinz Warneke made the plaster models for these carvings, which the stonecutters then replicated in the stone.

The center aisle ends at the chancel, where the organ is located. The console and pipes were made and installed by Joseph S. Whiteford of the Aeolian-Skinner Organ Company of Boston. The red-robed choir (the color was Mrs. Mellon's choice) performs in pews parallel to the aisle. There are two small rooms off the chancel. One is dedicated to floristry and the other is a sacristy where the rector and vestry prepare the communion and store their vestments.

On the south side of the chancel and altar are three double sets of arched stained-glass windows. Each portrays a saint or important ecclesiastical figure: Saint George; Saint Patrick, the "Apostle of Ireland"; Saint Augustine, the "Apostle to the English" and the first archbishop of Canterbury; the Venerable Bede, a monk who wrote the *Ecclesiastical History of the English People*; John Wycliffe, the "Morning star of the Reformation"; and Thomas Cranmer, archbishop of Canterbury, credited with the Book of Common Prayer and burned at the stake by order of Mary Tudor in 1556.

A cross constructed by Robert Hanback of rough-hewn barn timbers is nailed to the wall above the altar,

where parishioners receive the sacrament kneeling on blue needlepoint cushions. Gray Coyner recalls that Mrs. Mellon reacted decisively the day she walked into the church and saw the cross hanging on the wall for the first time. "That's it! We're not moving it."

The church was built during the Cold War, so a bomb shelter was installed in the basement and stocked with provisions for the community. The spacious area has since been converted into a room for the parish youth. One idiosyncratic feature was a consequence of Mrs. Mellon's insistence on fresh air: she rejected the installation of air conditioning. On one of the original blueprints, special instructions are written in longhand, "Omit all provision for future air conditioning." Fortunately for everyone concerned, the building was fully air-conditioned in the 1990s.

The exquisitely detailed wrought ironwork throughout the church—the bolts, hinges, nails, chandeliers, grilles, and railings—were designed and handcrafted by Paul J. Fiebiger and his metalwork firm, P. A. Fiebiger, in New York City (which later contributed to the restoration of the Statue of Liberty). Of particular note is the Angel of Peace, an exterior wall-mounted lantern that hangs on the south side of the church entrance. According to Joe Fiebiger, Paul Fiebiger's son, the design depicts "three angels that represent the angel Gabriel blowing his horn." The angels, he claims, are cast-bronze copies, handcrafted by his father, of the original eleventh-century Angel of Peace, which adorned a church in Wittichenau, Germany. Joe Fiebiger also maintains that the lantern was designed by H. Page Cross. The Angel of Peace was his father's gift to the Mellons, in keeping with the Fiebiger tradition of the artist acknowledging his gratitude to the patron. Paul Fiebiger told Reverend Cox, "Working on these things has been the greatest experience for us. For once we have been able to do our best, with no rush, no pressure. We have been allowed to be patient."

The weathervane atop the bell tower is an approximately five-foot-tall rooster. It was designed, cast in bronze, and covered with gold leaf by B. Eustbouts of the Netherlands. According to Joe Fiebiger, "The Mellons found the rooster during their travels in Holland and brought it to Trinity." Fiebiger recalls that his father

PAGE 164: The courtyard entrance of Trinity Episcopal Church in Upperville, Virginia.

PAGE 165: The stained-glass dedication window, which memorializes the Mellons' gift of the church buildings to Meade Parish.

PAGE 167: The cobblestone entrance to the cloister, which leads to the Mellon Close, as the family cemetery is called, and the outdoor chapel.

PAGE 168 TOP: One of the horse head–shaped door pulls on the entrance doors.

PAGE 168 BOTTOM: In the vestibule, the center beam is intentionally off-center.

PAGE 169: The nave and altar.

PAGE 170: The stained-glass windows in the nave illustrate stories from the Old and New Testaments, and the Apocrypha.

PAGE 171: The two stained-glass windows in the south transept, dated 1880–1919, are original to the second church building.

PAGE 173, CLOCKWISE FROM TOP LEFT: Oak pews carved with horticultural images; the hexagonal oak pulpit, hand carved by Heinz Warneke; carving of a Phoenix on the cap of a limestone pier; carving of a Unicorn.

OPPOSITE: The cross above the altar was constructed out of rough-hewn barn timbers by Robert Hanback.

TOP: Detail of the Angel of Peace lantern, located to the right of the entrance doors. It consists of three figures symbolizing the Angel Gabriel blowing his horn.

CENTER LEFT AND RIGHT: All of the wrought ironwork at Trinity Episcopal Church was designed and forged by the New York firm of P. A. Fiebiger.

BOTTOM LEFT: Bunny and Paul Mellon discovered the rooster weathervane in Holland.

BOTTOM RIGHT: A hackberry tree is prominently sited in the center of the circular courtyard. The parish hall is in the background.

"attached a simple ball bearing to the base of the rooster's support shaft to prevent it from squeaking when the wind blew." It is symbolic of the Christian's watchfulness and readiness for the return of Christ.

According to Katherine Wilkins, the trees on the church grounds were planted by Mrs. Mellon's arborist Clive Copenhaver. "Clive carried out her dreams," she says. When it came time to plant the large hackberry in the courtyard, "Clive planted the tree right where Mrs. Mellon wanted it. Then she stood back, studied the scene, and shook her head from side to side. 'It's not quite right, let's move it over a little.' They worked at it until it was right." Perry Wheeler collaborated with Mrs. Mellon on selecting many of the trees that were planted, including American holly, Sugar Tyme crab apple, *Magnolia* x *soulangeana* (saucer magnolia), tulip poplar, and western red cedar. Plans for a walled biblical garden as a place for contemplation were never realized.

In 1988 the Mellons deeded approximately thirty acres of their adjacent Skallerup Farm to Trinity for "ecumenical" use and to protect the view to the north. They later petitioned the church to establish a cemetery, which was consecrated on July 9, 1995. Mellon family graves were transferred from Rokeby to a separate section in the new cemetery that came to be called the Mellon Close. It is enclosed by a low stone wall and furnished with a stone bench for contemplation. Paul Mellon died in 1999 and was buried alongside other members of his family. The cemetery is not under church management and operates as a separate entity.

In 2012 an outdoor chapel was built as a place for "quiet meditation and occasional church services," Gray Coyner explains. It consists of a large cross in a council circle. And, "there is a fire pit and another council circle just below toward the creek."

Rachel Lambert Mellon's funeral service, "A Celebration of Life," was held at Trinity on March 28, 2014. Bouquets of white lilies adorned her casket, the vestibule, and the altar. The congregation sang the hymns "Oh God, Our Help in Ages Past" and "In the Bleak Midwinter." The Gospel reading was from John 14:1–6, and Reverend Robert L. Banse Jr., Rector of Trinity, delivered the

OPPOSITE: The cemetery is located on the north side of the church grounds.

ABOVE: The Mellon Close, where Bunny and Paul Mellon and other members of the Mellon and Lloyd families are buried.

RIGHT: The cross and council circle of the outdoor chapel.

PAGES 178–79: The south façade of the church, featuring the east-facing Mellon dedication window in the south transept.

PAGES 180–81: The bell tower of Trinity Episcopal Church rises above the autumn foliage.

homily. The American Boychoir, whose longtime home had once been Albemarle, Mrs. Mellon's childhood home in Princeton, New Jersey, sang Bay Psalm 23, and Bette Midler sang "The Rose."

The committal followed in the churchyard cemetery. On the front of the tombstone, an image of an oak tree is chiseled above the inscription:

RACHEL LAMBERT MELLON

9 AUG 1910

17 MAR 2014

THE LORD IS MY SHEPHERD

On the back of the tombstone, a cross and the words of a Bible verse are chiseled in the stone. It reads: "The wind bloweth where it listeth, and thou heareth the sound thereof, but canst not tell whence it cometh, and whither it goeth: so is every one that is born of the Spirit. John III, 8." Buried at her side are her son and daughter, Stacy Barcroft Lloyd III and Eliza Lloyd Moore.

Father Banse says that some people refer to Trinity as the Mellon church. But when he was first invited to the Mellons' house, Bunny asked him if it was okay for her to come to his church to pray. He replied, "Of course, but it's not my church—it's God's church."

Every Christmas, J. D. Tutwiler, Bunny's long-trusted gardener at Oak Spring, observes the time-honored tradition of crafting wreaths for the Mellon graves. Mrs. Mellon's wreath is a ring of boxwood ornamented with holly berries, slices of citrus, pinecones, and bits of bracken fronds from her Oak Spring garden.

In December 2004 Mrs. Mellon's friend Bryan Huffman visited Trinity during the first week of Advent and remembered seeing cedar trees leaning in the corners, "adorned with nothing but their raw, natural beauty." The tradition continues to this day. Inside the church, four unadorned cedars are casually propped up against the upper corners of the chancel and the nave. A large Advent wreath formed of boxwood from the churchyard and with candles aglow is placed near the south transept. The altar is draped in blue for the Christmas season services. Simple adornments in Mrs. Mellon's style. "We honor her," Gray Coyner says softly.

Mellon Family Gardens

NEW YORK CITY

The house at 125 East 70th Street in New York City was a home away from home for the Mellons. Bunny had been born in the city and Paul, a Pittsburgh native, visited frequently during his formative years. In 1935 he and his first wife, Mary Conover Brown, rented a brownstone on the same site. Thirty years later, long after he and Bunny married, they leveled that brownstone and the one next to it and commissioned H. Page Cross to design a six-floor, L-shaped, 11,000-square-foot house. Forty feet wide and one hundred feet deep, it was more than twice the usual size of a New York townhouse. The exterior of the house was initially painted mustard yellow. French Provincial in style, it featured arched doorways, a Juliette balcony with a curved wrought-iron railing, louvered window shutters, French doors, a dormered mansard roof, and a walled-in garden. Paul Goldberger, architectural critic for the *New York Times* in the 1970s, loved its "wedding-cake charm," and the *AIA Guide to New York City* described it as "anachronistic; a charming stuccoed confection of French provincial that France itself never experienced."

With exposures on three sides—south, east, and north—high ceilings, and an abundance of windows, the house was filled with light. Mrs. Mellon considered natural light an essential element of design and wrote in her journal of the importance of creating "walls for the light to bounce off of."

A wall concealed the south-facing entrance courtyard from passersby. Each spring, a tree on city property in front of the townhouse would burst into a riot of white flowers, a perfect example of Mrs. Mellon's principle of taking advantage of the "borrowed" landscape. Planted in the courtyard, in front of the staff/service entrance to the right of the main entrance, was a cherry tree that reached the second-floor. A wrought-iron fence and gate, hand forged by Paul Fiebiger, who had crafted all the ironwork at Trinity Episcopal Church, separated the two entrances. A bas-relief of an oak tree, the emblem of Oak Spring, was carved in the keystone of the archway over black double front doors at the main entrance, which was flanked by two crab apple trees. The doors opened onto a corridor that led past a powder room—its yellow walls hand painted in a garden trellis design—to the back of the house, where the hallway leading out to the garden was paneled in lattice and filled with baskets from Mrs. Mellon's collection. Indeed, Bunny introduced garden motifs throughout the interior, striking a balance between elegance and comfort. Mr. Mellon's library, located on the first floor at the back of the house, opened onto the walled garden, which was surrounded by low-rise townhouses.

Bunny designed the garden with landscape architect Perry Wheeler, her dear friend and frequent collaborator. The trees included magnolias, hardy oranges, and honey locusts, as well as a holly tree near the back door, all favorites of Mrs. Mellon. The ground was paved in squares of a white-and-gray stone with diamond-shaped inlays of slate-gray stone. The central feature was a rectangular bed planted with ivy and surrounded by a boxwood hedge. Four eighteenth-century Italian obelisks marked the corners. A trelliswork gazebo with a fleur-de-lis finial adorned the northeast corner. Beds along the walls were filled with Kingsville boxwood, azaleas, and seasonal flowers. The ripened fruit of a quince tree espaliered on

the back wall would often fall into the neighboring yard. According to Claire White, who owned the townhouse after the Mellons, the neighbor's housekeeper would make quince jam with the fruit that had fallen from the tree. A stand of trees along the north wall grew in perfect alignment. The Oak Spring garden department was on site twice a month, and the tree department tended the trees at least four times a year. The honey locusts and magnolias eventually outgrew the space and had to be removed.

The media/family room was on the second floor, as were a study, the kitchen, a breakfast room, and a laundry. The cherry tree in the courtyard unfurled its pink blossoms in the spring, right outside the kitchen window. "We ate our breakfast at that window with a veritable aviary on the nearby branches," recalls Claire White.

On the third floor, both the south-facing dining room and the east-facing drawing room opened onto an expansive terrace, measuring eighteen feet wide by thirty-four feet long. A tall, intricately patterned trellis running the entire length of the terrace along its eastern edge, concealed the brick wall of the neighboring townhouse, turning what could have been an eyesore into an object of beauty. Versailles tubs planted with holly trees lined the balustrade along the southern, street-facing edge to afford privacy.

Bunny hired John Fowler and his assistant, Imogen Taylor, of the British design firm Colefax and Fowler to decorate the interior of the house. Fowler was not interested in crossing the Atlantic, so he managed the project by mail, sending sketches and fabric swatches to Paul Leonard and William Strom, Bunny's New York employees, who executed the design. The drawing room was cozy, warm, and inviting, with walls painted a peachy pink. John Singer Sargent's *Miss Beatrice Townsend*, 1882, hung over the fireplace, which was elaborately carved with garden imagery, including gardening tools, flowers, and birds. A jeweled tree by Jean Schlumberger rested on the mantel.

In the dining room, the walls were painted a vibrant cobalt blue in a crosshatch pattern to add a sense of texture. Édouard Manet's *George Moore in the Artist's Garden*, ca. 1879, hung between a pair of French doors. And two

graceful little herb trees, meticulously pruned by Bunny herself, stood on small tables in front of the windows. "She had a good handshake—strong hands and a good grip—from all that pruning!" Bryan Huffman recalls. Wide panels in the walls opened to reveal cabinets in which table linens were stored. Beautifully embroidered with garden motifs, including the oak tree emblem of Oak Spring, many were designed by Hubert de Givenchy and Philippe Venet. The wood floor was hand painted in a floral pattern in the center of the room and a geometric pattern on the periphery.

Two master suites occupied the fourth floor, and both overlooked the terrace. Mrs. Mellon's suite featured a balcony. A back stair, accessible from her suite, provided secondary access to all the floors. There were three guest rooms on the fifth floor, and the sixth housed the building systems and storage space. A wine cellar, a laundry, and more storage rooms were on the basement level.

When in New York, the Mellons entertained frequently and explored the art market, looking for paintings to add to their collection. Bunny encouraged Paul's interest in French artists. As Mr. Mellon wrote in his autobiography: "Bunny's imagination and visual acuity have influenced me. It is not widely enough known that she is an amateur landscapist and gardener (although of professional capability), and her theories of landscape and of proportion in architecture (she reads blueprints far better than I) have certainly enlarged my own "interior" landscapes, as well as having educated me considerably while we pursued our joint venture of collecting French paintings."

For a time, New York was the epicenter of their universe, but as life moved on, so did they, spending more time in Washington, D.C., and at Oak Spring, where they enjoyed the pursuits nearest to their hearts—Paul, his horses, and Bunny, her garden.

{ MELLON FAMILY GARDENS }

PAGES 182–83: The view of Half Moon Bay from King's Leap, the Mellon family home on Antigua.

PAGE 184: Bunny and Paul Mellon's New York townhouse at 125 East 70th Street.

PAGE 185: An oak tree, the emblem of Oak Spring, hand embroidered on linen.

PAGE 186: The main entrance courtyard. A bas-relief of an oak tree is carved into the keystone of the archway above the double front doors.

PAGE 188: The hallway leading to the garden was lined in lattice and filled with a selection of baskets from Bunny's collection.

PAGE 189: A rectangular bed of ivy, bordered by a boxwood hedge and punctuated by obelisks at the corners, was the central feature in the garden.

PAGES 190–91: The 18-by-34-foot terrace off the drawing room and dining room on the third floor features a trellis that obscures the brick wall of the neighboring townhouse.

TOP LEFT: John Singer Sargent's *Miss Beatrice Townsend*, 1882, hung over the fireplace in the peachy pink drawing room.

BOTTOM LEFT: In the blue-walled, light-filled dining room, Édouard Manet's *George Moore in the Artist's Garden*, ca.1879, has pride of place.

OPPOSITE: A selection of Bunny's hand-embroidered linens.

CAPE COD

An American flag was hoisted up the flagpole to signal that Paul and Bunny Mellon had arrived at their Cape Cod estate in Oyster Harbors, an island connected by a bridge to Osterville. The Mellons built the Main House and gardens in the late 1950s on a bluff overlooking the Seapuit River. At Bunny's direction, the gardens were integrated into the surrounding landscape. The whole effect was graceful and harmonious. "We live by the sea," she wrote in her garden instructions. "So the sea as far as your eye can reach is part of the small piece of land you own. What you do with this land takes in the sea. Or not." The site had an expansive view that included the river, a barrier reef called Dead Neck Island, Nantucket Sound, and all the summer sailboat traffic. • Cape Cod is paradise in summer, perfect for an outdoor lifestyle, but it's not the easiest place to cultivate a garden. Nature has the final say in its success or failure. Cool summer temperatures, sandy soil, salt air, gale-force winds, and hurricanes that contribute to beach and dune erosion represent the major challenges to designing a successful and enduring garden. Mrs. Mellon noted in her garden journal, "There are so many things to be gained by asking questions first. Where does the wind come from that is harsh in winter, and in summer where does the house cast shadows?"

The estate comprised several houses: the Main House, where the Main Garden was located; the Dune House, her private getaway; and Putnam House, one of the oldest homes on the Cape and reserved for family. The property was surrounded by a bit of everything: beach, dunes, meadows, and pine forests, all connected by a network of tidy sandy paths.

By the time the morning light indicated "VII" on the sundial in the Main Garden, the day's work had begun. On the Cape, the ocean was their centerpiece, but the day revolved around food. The gardener, basket in hand, began the morning ritual, a walk along the grassy paths in the Main Garden to gather the herbs, fruits, and vegetables that would be incorporated into the menu for the day. Favorite herbs were snipped: basil, chives, parsley, tarragon, and sorrel. (One prized menu from family friend and occasional personal chef Rudolph Stanish, "the Omelet King," included not omelets but sorrel soup, roast beef, popovers, squash, salad, and chocolate mousse.)

The vegetables included beets, carrots, cucumbers, lettuce, lima beans, onions, squash, zucchini, and tomatoes. Mr. Mellon often asked, "Is this one of those tomatoes that cost me a thousand dollars?" Among the pure delights of summer was a sandwich with one of those thousand-dollar tomatoes: "Peel and slice a tomato. Drain on paper towel. Trim off the crust of two slices of thin white bread. Spread a very thin layer of mayonnaise on each slice of bread. Layer tomatoes on one slice of bread, sprinkle with salt and pepper, place second slice on top and cut in half."

A bushel basket overflowing with apples, peaches, plums, and other delicious offerings was brought in from the orchard and carried to the washing pavilion on the south side of the Main Garden, where the fruit was cleaned and readied for the kitchen. Fruit was almost always included on the day's menus. It was sauced, sliced, and stewed into cakes, compotes, ice cream, jellies, pies, and tarts. And sometimes it was simply served fresh.

Another basket was filled with cut flowers for the house. The selection might include purple and white cosmos, daisies, delphiniums, marigolds, snapdragons, and zinnias. The tiniest stems were tucked into miniature inkwell bottles for display on bedroom nightstands and dressing tables.

Gift baskets of fresh herbs, flowers, and vegetables were prepared to share with family, friends, and neighbors. The rest of the day's harvest was placed in the pantry refrigerator. The housekeeper discussed the day's menus with Bunny at the conclusion of breakfast and before the morning swim. The menu options were handwritten on Osterville letterhead in memorandum format, with the Mellons humorously referring to themselves as "Prisoner 2a" and "Prisoner 2b" and the housekeeper as "Warden." For example, on August 10, 1996, the lunch menu included: Corn on the Cob, Corned Beef Hash, and Green Salad with Beets, Sliced Tomatoes, Eggs—stuffed, Cucumber/Cream Cheese Sandwich, and Melon. For dinner there was a choice: Madrilene, B.L.T., Chicken Sandwich, Ham Sandwich or Omelette. Bunny circled her selection, "Omelette," and signed it "2b."

On one menu the Warden wrote, "Have a nice day!!" and 2b wrote back, "Same to the Warden. 2a must be out on parole." On another menu the Warden again wrote, "Have a nice day," and 2a wrote back, "You 2." Prison-themed doodles often decorated the menus: a pair of feet in chains, a coffee cup behind bars, and a compliment from 2b: "Excellent prison fare!"

When the garden crew arrived, work began in earnest: planting, pruning, seed sowing, transplanting, and the daily scouring of a large sunken birdbath, as well as polishing the sundial, dead-heading the plants, and tedious weeding, which was done by hand. No mulch. To combat the dry spells that are typical of the Cape in high summer, an army of oscillating water sprinklers was rotated around the gardens and sometimes ran the better part of the day.

About one o'clock Paul and Bunny made their way down the sandy path to what they referred to as their beach house, which was more cabana than house, for lunch—and

to be out of earshot. For that is when the gardeners began their labor-intensive mowing. All mowing was done with twenty-one-inch power lawn mowers to keep the noise to a minimum—very important to Mr. Mellon. It took hours to complete the mowing, and it was a tricky business because Bunny wanted a country farm look and an overall natural feel. That meant allowing the grass to grow tall—but only to a point. Besides, the rabbits needed a place to live too.

The trees were a valued component of the landscape and had a dedicated gardener. Bobby Childs, the "Tree Man," enjoyed a bird's-eye view of the estate as he pruned the trees. It was very important that the trees were pruned—not manicured—and shaped to harmonize with the gently rolling terrain. The autumn olive and Russian olive, with their silvery foliage, were among the smaller tree varieties Bunny enjoyed. Sometimes the trees were living sculptures and sometimes they weren't. One day she asked Bobby to trim some branches that were blocking the view from a window. When he hesitated, the request was repeated. But still

he hesitated, knowing better than to ignore the "three times rule" that Lisa Rockwell, the head gardener, had instituted: "Never cut *anything* until Mrs. Mellon says it three times." Not adhering to this hard-and-fast rule could be a quick way to lose one's job. So, when Bobby explained to Mrs. Mellon that he wasn't supposed to cut anything until she had said it three times, she offered a suggestion: "Bobby, then you pretend that branch is one of Mr. Mellon's lawyers!"

The Main House had panoramic seaward views. In front of it was a grass terrace dotted with irregular pieces of stone in a random checkerboard pattern. A crescent-shaped flower garden filled with daisies, dusty miller, petunias, salvia, and sunflowers wrapped around the terrace. There was also an herb wheel planted with a variety of herbs between the spokes: parsley, savory, tarragon, chives, lemon verbena, cilantro, marjoram, bronze fennel, sage, and thyme.

The Main Garden was a large rectangular space, not quite half an acre, surrounded by a privet hedge. The hedge was clipped to a height of four feet, low enough so as not

to obscure the view and high enough to provide a natural buffer from the winds off the sea. The hedge created a microclimate conducive to plant cultivation and was pretty to look at. It was a Martha Washington–style garden, meant to supply food for the family table. And its location close to the house made the kitchen deliveries easier.

Before the garden was planted, the earth was dug to a depth of four feet and filled with Barnstable loam (locally enriched farm soil). Lisa Rockwell says the soil was tested every "blue moon" and supplemented with dehydrated manure and a general all-purpose fertilizer. There was a stand of birch trees behind the garden and a glorious English oak nearby. A small building with weathered shingles in the traditional one-and-a-half-story Cape Cod style, called the Head House, faced west and anchored the far side of the garden. It served as a work space/office for the gardeners and became the architectural focal point of the garden. Flanking it were two Lord & Burnham greenhouses, where hundreds of annuals were propagated every year and used to replenish the garden throughout the seasons. The greenhouses, in turn, were flanked by two octagonal pavilions in the Mount Vernon "pepper-pot" style, as Dean

Norton, Mount Vernon's director of horticulture, calls it. The pavilion on the north side was used for drying herbs and flowers; it featured an ingenious revolving ladder that reached up to the curved wooden ceiling to make the drying pegs accessible. The pavilion on the south side, closer to the kitchen of the Main House, was equipped with a sink and counter space and was used to prepare the produce for the kitchen. In front of the Head House, a brick terrace, ornamented with white alyssum and a single Red Stayman apple tree, provided a clean transitional space from the work centers to the garden, and the warm afternoon sunshine made it a great place to begin the gradual process of moving the plants outdoors by introducing them to direct sunlight during the day and cool temperatures at night.

The garden began at the front entrance gates and ended at the Head House. It was divided into twelve rectangular and square beds that were laid out in three equally spaced, lengthwise rows that ran east to west, separated by two grass pathways. Each row was comprised of four planting beds. Three grass paths ran crosswise, north to south, each intersecting the lengthwise paths at two points. At one of the intersecting

PAGE 194: A sailboat glides along the Seapuit River, which fronts the Mellon family's Cape Cod estate. In the distance is the barrier reef Dead Neck Island and, beyond that, Nantucket Sound.

PAGE 195: Bunny's watercolor of Nantucket Sound.

PAGE 197: A flower and herb garden at Putnam House, one of the residences on the estate.

PAGE 198: The terrace at Dune House, overlooking the swimming pool, the Seapuit River, Dead Neck Island, and Nantucket Sound.

PAGE 199: The children's playhouse, seen from the dining room of the Main House.

PAGE 200: An overview of the Main Garden.

PAGE 201, CLOCKWISE FROM TOP LEFT: The Head House—the gardeners' work space and office—flanked by greenhouses; Bunny's herb trees soaking up the sun in one of the greenhouses; wildflowers cover the Field near Dune House; the washing pavilion and one of the grassy paths dividing the flower beds in the Main Garden; the lush summer landscape.

OPPOSITE: A garden of perennials at Putnam House.

TOP RIGHT: The washing pavilion in the Main Garden, where the fruits and vegetables were prepared for the kitchen.

BOTTOM RIGHT: A corner picnic shelter in the Dune House herb garden.

PAGE 204: A flourishing fruit tree espaliered on the fence in the Dune House garden.

PAGE 207: A crescent-shaped flower garden rims the stone-paved terrace overlooking the water at the Main House.

{ MELLON FAMILY GARDENS }

points in the center crosswise path there was a circular birdbath and at the other, a sundial.

In the planting beds on the north side, sixty to seventy straight rows of vegetables were planted in the spring every year in two rectangular beds. A twenty-foot-long trellis perpendicular to the drying pavilion was dedicated to those pricey tomatoes, including Sweet 100 cherry tomatoes, Better Boy, Big Girl, Early Pick VF Hybrid, and Lady Luck. The trellis provided not only support for the tomatoes but also protection from deer, rabbits, and other opportunists. Basil, carrots, and marigolds, natural friends of tomatoes, were planted in and around the tomato cage, taking advantage of their symbiosis to help repel pests and attract beneficial insects.

Planted along the trellis were borders of tuberoses and lady's mantle. To contrast the bright colors and make them pop, plants in light and airy shades of gray were mixed in. Among Mrs. Mellon's favorite gray-colored plants were *Artemisia* 'Powis Castle', dusty miller 'Silver Dust', and *Artemisia ludoviciana* 'Silver King'.

The two beds closest to the front gate in the middle row were filled with hot-colored zinnias (Giant Wine, Gumdrop, Oriole, Purple Prince, Queen Red Lime, White Wedding, and Zahara Mix) and Old World shrub roses planted in clusters. A mix of herbs bordered the bed. The crosswise path between the first two center beds was bordered with roses. The palette was white, pale pink, and pale yellow. Mrs. Mellon's rose collection included fifty beloved John F. Kennedy greenish white hybrid tea roses, the center of each planted one foot away from the center of the next, along with clusters of such cultivars as 'Nastarana', 'Felicia', 'White Pet', 'Wife of Bath', 'Iceberg', Austin 'The Prince', 'Madame Pierre Oger', 'Sharifa Asma', and 'Fisherman's Friend'.

The two beds in the middle row closest to the Head House were divided into four smaller beds by a center path that connected to the terrace in front of the Head House and two crosswise paths. These four beds had petal-shaped centers filled with *Rudbeckia hirta* 'Prairie Sun', commonly known as black-eyed Susan, which were surrounded by Daddy Blue petunias, *Nicotiana* 'Saratoga White', *Gomphrena globosa* 'Woodcreek Purple', salvia

seascape, and Mrs. Mellon's beloved Scotch roses. The two outside beds, corner squares that bordered the washing and drying pavilions, were sliced by pathways into triangles and planted with a variety of flowers in blocks of color.

After April 15 every year Lisa Rockwell began planting the vegetable beds on the south side of the garden, though the start date was always dependent on the weather. There were double rows of lima beans, spinach, peas, carrots, and sorrel followed by dill, kuta squash, peppers, and beets. Cauliflower, broccoli, scallions, onions, and shallots were grouped in the middle and at the ends of the beds. Romaine, Red Sails, and Great Lakes lettuces bordered the beds and wide swaths of Shasta daisies filled the corners.

To bring charm and height to the beds closest to the washing pavilion, two sweet pea towers were planted with Fragrantissima and King Size Navy Blue in colors of lavender, white, blue, and salmon. Two beds were filled with a variety of perennials that changed through the years, including Ada Ballard, Eventide and Frikartii asters; Everest, Caroline van den Berg, and Progress phlox; *Liatris scariosa*; columbine; delphiniums; Gypsophila; and *Stokesia laevis* 'Alba'.

In 1992 vegetable production was cut back and the front half of the garden was turned into an orchard of plum, apple, peach, and cherry trees: Fellenberg and Greengage plums; Red and Yellow Delicious, Duchess of Oldenburg, Honeycrisp, Maiden Blush, Sheepnose, and Smokehouse apples; Reliance, Redhaven, and Hale-Haven peaches; North Star and Stella Sweet cherries. The gardeners searched high and low for the Sheepnose apple variety and after successfully locating it, learned at first bite that it was a storage apple, not to be eaten until all the other apples in the cellar were gone, giving the sugars time to sweeten up.

At the Dune House, the terrace was densely planted with white alyssum and *Lobelia* in cobalt and Cambridge blue. The herb garden, bordered by boxwood and santolina hedges, was planted with Italian white sunflowers, mother of thyme, oregano, and lavender. The flowers were fashioned into herb wreaths and carried to the drying pavilion in the Main Garden, where they were hung to dry.

Near the Dune House was the dune-filled Field, which ultimately became covered with wildflowers. The project began when Mrs. Mellon decided to plant a splash of red Shirley poppies in the field. Organic matter, including compost and humus, was added to the sandy soil, the grass was eradicated, milkweed was planted, and the space was seeded by hand with white daisies, blue lupine, and native perennial sedges that resemble grasses and thrive in damp soil. Even the Field was treated as a bona fide garden and had a yearly maintenance schedule. A woodshed was built for aesthetic effect, not practicality. With its classic construction and whitewashed exterior, it added a rustic focal point to the view.

Mrs. Mellon brought a spirit of adventure to her gardens and loved to be surprised by different combinations. Wanting them to look as if "God had created it," she welcomed the appearance of volunteer plants, which she felt added interest and appeal, and she instructed the gardeners not to weed them. She encouraged the gardeners to feel free to try new things, but there was no mincing of words when the surprises fell flat. One season the phlox variety *Phlox drummondii*, or Phlox of Sheep, was propagated. It features delicate flowers in a blend of pastel colors and typically grows to about a foot tall. When the phlox had been transplanted, Mrs. Mellon took one look and commented that it reminded her of "old ladies' underwear." The phlox was gone minutes later.

For Mrs. Mellon, gardens were living canvases, and she would change the floral emphasis annually, so there was always something new to see. The Cape Cod gardens would begin to take shape by the end of June. Flower pots were planted with beach grasses, *Lobelia*, heliotrope, and lemon geranium. And there were plant tubs of morning glories, *Thunbergia*, cardinal climbers, and delphiniums. Someone remarked to Mrs. Mellon that she would not be able to grow delphiniums in the Cape's climate, to which she replied, "Watch me!" And she did. The Italian white sunflowers made excellent cutting flowers and attracted butterflies and yellow finches that would flit and dart around the garden.

The Mellons' Cape Cod estate, situated in Massachusetts's wetlands, was subject to the state's strict environ-mental laws, and this became an issue when Bunny decided to create a garden on Dead Neck Island. In her journal she wrote that she had "always wanted to do a garden on a barrier reef," and Dead Neck Island, within direct sight of her home and her view of the ocean, was exactly that. She wanted the garden to have a soft, natural look. Anything dark green had to be removed, particularly the rugosa roses, which she believed contributed to beach erosion. Knowing that the state would probably never give permission, and feeling that the Mellons had paid their fair share of taxes, the gardeners took matters into their own hands. One night they rode their boats over to Dead Neck Island, cleared the offending plants from the island, and carried the clippings and debris in their boats back to shore, burning the evidence in their "midnight bonfires."

The gardeners always knew when Mrs. Mellon was in residence. Before they saw her, they would catch a whiff of Givenchy III on the wind and then discover her lovingly tending the plants with her own set of tools. But over the years, as her abilities waned and her eyesight weakened, simply being in the garden was enough for her. Perhaps Paul Mellon said it best in one of his delightful poems:

A FAMILY GATHERING AT OYSTER HARBORS

Now that we're all together
In our twenty-first year at Cape Cod
(Some who are light as a feather
Some covered with avoirdupoid)
Here's a toast from all those
Who are grateful
For our years in the sun
And the sea,
And another . . . a gallon, a tankful
To one, for all she has done
To whom we're all love full and thankful
To our own horticultural Bun.

NANTUCKET

The Mellons' Nantucket estate—approximately 210 acres purchased in March 1969—was located in Forked Pond Valley on the island's southern shore. It was reached by traveling due east on Milestone Road toward the quaint village of Siasconset and turning south onto an unpaved track through sand-plain grasslands. According to Jim Lentowski, executive director of the Nantucket Conservation Foundation, Mrs. Mellon wanted to move a portion of a road in which they had a common interest. It was a "logical repositioning," Jim remembers. He characterized her as a "landscape painter." She did paint with watercolors, but mostly she painted with plants. "She moved elements of the landscape around that were very natural." • The entrance to the estate was simple—a gate flanked by a split-rail fence and a sign that read "Slowly Please Blind Corner Ahead." Boulders extracted from the fields lined both sides of the beginning of the driveway. The parcel, a relatively flat outwash plain of dense scrub oak thickets was subject

to seasonal storm surges and hostile to gardens—and gardeners—presenting formidable challenges. The main house and a complex of service buildings were originally built on a bluff overlooking Tom Nevers Head, where the island's old whaling lookout station had been located. The modest Cape Cod–style structures followed the Island's rigid design rules and regulations for rooflines: gables with a minimum 7 in 12 inch pitch and a maximum 12 in 12 inch pitch; shed roofs with a minimum 4 in 12 inch pitch. The casement windows were inward swinging with true divided lights. From the house one could appreciate the open pastureland and watch as the strong ocean currents rearranged the shoreline. Eventually, erosion threatened the stability of the structures and the complex was moved inland. The first small building Mrs. Mellon constructed on the property was a picnic house. The architect came, listened, and built it, only to be told to tear it down. A second was built and it, too, was torn down. The third attempt was finally the charm.

A model airplane club on the island asked Mrs. Mellon if they could use a field north of her house to fly their noisy remote-control planes. The field was wide open and remote. She agreed to the arrangement as long as they promised to stay organized and manage their aircraft. The locals jokingly referred to the field as Lambert Field after her family's St. Louis Lambert International Airport. She made provisions in her will for the club to continue to fly the planes over her property after her death. Much of the estate itself was bequeathed to the Nantucket Conservation Foundation.

Trees were an important component of all Mrs. Mellon's landscapes, but on Nantucket it was nearly impossible to cultivate her favorite specimens. The wintry gales and salt spray depleted the soil, sculpted the terrain, and wreaked havoc on any landscape plans. She nevertheless planted shadbush, or serviceberry, trees (the name derives from the fish because the tree is in full bloom when the shad run). "A dead fish was tucked Squanto-style under the roots of every tree," says Neil

Peterson, who worked her land for more than thirty years. The trees didn't survive. She planted hawthorns, too, but they didn't survive either.

One technique that Mrs. Mellon had been fond of over the years was to place wooden tree-shaped forms in trial planting sites so that she could observe shade and shadows. In Nantucket the idea of a wooden tree form took on new life, and trees modeled after hawthorns were fabricated, painted white, and sited around the property, mostly close to the house. They lent a sense of shelter, served as windbreaks, and added a visual element to punctuate the view of the horizon.

Other projects included farming, and it was probably the first time in many years that hay was made on the property. She also hoped to reclaim the landscape and return it to native grasses, but to do so required the land to be cleared—a lengthy (it would take years!), grueling process. Gradually, portions of the scrub oak were cleared and planted with grass seedlings.

The storm systems were punishing and often laid waste to the landscape. Snow fencing that served as a defense often became tangled like a necklace chain and had to be straightened out and repositioned. The winds tossed the sand about, widening the beach in some places and narrowing it in others. "She was understanding when disasters happened, compassionate to those around her," Neil Paterson recalls.

A small, enclosed garden, tended by Lisa Rockwell, was sited near the house. It was accessed by a stone walkway with alyssum growing in the stone's cracks. The surrounding wall provided shelter from the wind and salt spray coming off the Atlantic. Three raised beds lined the walls. The beds in two of the corners curved around crab apple trees, which thrived thanks to the protection of the wall. These beds were planted with Queen Margrethe and Othello roses, as well as several David Austin specimens: soft yellow Windrush, rosy pink Wife of Bath, and fragrant, dark red Fisherman's Friend. Also

planted in the raised beds were other flowers, herbs, and vegetables: bee balm, chamomile, cosmos, dill, tarragon, Sweet 100 tomatoes, yarrow (including, 'Apple Blossom', 'Salmon Beauty', 'The Beacon', and 'Great Expectations', all obtained from Wayside Gardens' Achillea Galaxy Collection), and large and small zinnias. A two-foot-wide walkway provided access to the beds.

At one time there were two symmetrical rectangular beds in the center of the garden. One was an herb garden planted with parsley, sweet marjoram, basil and chives. The other was filled with Patio tomatoes, small- and large-leaf basil, and loose-leaf lettuce. It was edged with her favorite alyssum. Bush cucumbers were grown in two pots.

Mrs. Mellon was pleased with the progress in the Nantucket garden and always looked forward to the next season. After the winter ritual of poring over the colorful plant and seed catalogue "wish books," she would pen a few instructions and suggestions for Lisa Rockwell: "Could you plant peppers (new orange color), cucumbers

'Salad Bush,' oak leaf lettuce, dwarf cosmos, and Fino Verde Basil." Always something new.

The stated mission of the Nantucket Conservation Foundation is to "assist in the preservation of Nantucket's character by permanently conserving, maintaining and managing natural areas and habitats and to encourage an appreciation of and interest in the island's natural resources." In recent decades, Nantucket has flourished as a vacation destination, and the "impact of population growth has been keenly felt in high-density development," says Jim Lentowski. Wanting to place a portion of her land under protection, Mrs. Mellon quite naturally reached out to the foundation. "She held dear to her love of the land," Lentowski says. Of her original 210 acres, she bequeathed 107 acres to the foundation. This gift completed an assemblage of 2,150 acres, known as Madequecham and Tom Nevers, a prairie-like ecosystem. Writing about Nantucket in his autobiography, *Reflections in a Silver Spoon*, Paul Mellon commented that Bunny "loves to hear the waves beating

PAGE 208: Bunny makes adjustments to a wooden "tree" fabricated in the form of a hawthorn near her enclosed garden on Nantucket. She resorted to wooden tree forms because the punishing climate on the island prohibited the cultivation of her favorite species.

PAGE 209: Bunny's watercolor of two of her favorite subjects: sea and sky.

PAGE 210: Bunny's distinctive fence-painting technique began with a base of dirty yellow streaked with grays, browns, white, and raw umber.

PAGE 211: After the original house was relocated farther inland, new garden walls were built and a new garden was designed. Bunny wanted things to *look* old, not *be* old.

PAGE 212: The walls protected the garden from the stormy blasts and severe winds that swept across the pasture, permitting the planting of flowers, herbs, and vegetables along the walls and in rectangular beds in the center.

PAGE 213: The new garden overlooked the South Pasture.

BELOW: Wildflowers cover the South Pasture in early summer.

RIGHT: The rugged beauty of the South Pasture in late summer.

on the shore with the same rhythm and deep roar that she remembers from her early days." And he was aware that "much of her land will eventually belong to the Nantucket Conservation Foundation for its perpetual preservation." Though her beachfront property is open to the public today, the dense thickets of eight- to ten-foot-high scrub oak and pitch pine make it inaccessible. As Mrs. Mellon would say in her understated way, "That will need attention." The conservation restrictions will preserve its natural beauty and it will forever be home to the white-tailed deer and the wildflowers.

{ MELLON FAMILY GARDENS }

ANTIGUA

Every year, Paul and Bunny Mellon celebrated Christmas at Oak Spring and then flew to King's Leap, their villa on Antigua in the West Indies, for the winter season. "After Christmas, Bunny and I usually leave for Antigua with a few friends or family members," Paul Mellon penned in his autobiography, *Reflections in a Silver Spoon*. "There is a landing strip on the farm that accommodates our Gulf . . . so it is just a matter of driving to it and leaving the cold weather behind." There were three flagpoles lining the landing strip: the Stars and Stripes was flown on one, the national flag of guests on the second (usually the British Union Jack or the French tricolor), and the Rokeby Stables gray-and-yellow standard with its sheaf-of-wheat emblem ("always flown when I am returning from a winning race," Mr. Mellon wrote) on the third. • Antigua, located in the Leeward Islands of the eastern Caribbean, is roughly circular in shape: fourteen miles wide and twelve miles long. Its 108-square-mile land mass is comprised of limestone highlands

{ MELLON FAMILY GARDENS }

in the northeast, a central plain, and volcanic mountains in the southwest. Its jagged, ninety-five-mile-long coastline features pink-tinged white sandy beaches, coral reefs, and natural harbors. During the eighteenth century the production of sugarcane was the mainstay of the island's economy, but today it is tourism. Locally grown fruits and vegetables include avocados, baby bananas, coconuts, corn, cucumbers, mangoes, okra, and pineapples.

The Mellons were founding members of the Mill Reef Club, an exclusive winter retreat launched in the late 1940s by Robertson "Happy" Ward. He converted a 1,500-acre parcel of abandoned sugarcane farmland along Antigua's eastern coast into a private enclave of homes designed in unpretentious architectural styles that were comfortable, informal, and embraced the natural beauty of the island. At the time Antigua was primitive; there was no electricity or running water. Transportation around the island was sketchy at best. Travelers aboard the "Mill Reef Special," Pan Am's weekly flight from New York, were greeted at the airport in the island spirit with a rum punch and the calypso and reggae stylings of a steel band, but from there it was a rough ride across the terrain on mostly unpaved roads. The seclusion of Mill Reef is what appealed to the Mellons. "To me, privacy is the most valuable asset that money can buy," Paul Mellon wrote in his autobiography. One of the island's national parks borders the club property, and its amenities eventually included a hotel, a clubhouse, tennis courts, and a golf course.

For Mr. Mellon, Mill Reef came to signify much more than the name of a private club. In the late 1960s he "bred a classic horse" and called it Mill Reef. "It was a great horse," he wrote, "whose name would always rank among the highest in the annals of racing" following a legendary career. "The name Mill Reef is taken from a winter club and a beautiful stretch of sea near our house in Antigua, in the West Indies." The horse and the home in Mill Reef were both big winners for the Mellons.

King's Leap was a three-level complex nestled into the hillside. It was designed by family friend H. Page Cross. The twenty-seven-acre property commanded breathtaking views of crescent-shaped Half Moon Bay—arguably one of the prettiest bays in the world—and sloped down

to pristine sandy beaches and clear turquoise waters. Temperatures range in the seventies and eighties year round. "There is an indescribable feeling of peace with the warm air softly cooled by the trade winds," Mr. Mellon wrote. The atmosphere was casual and relaxed. Mr. Mellon walked around barefoot and in shorts with a beach towel thrown over his shoulder. And he got work done, too, typing his own correspondence.

"The house itself is reminiscent of an old West Indian plantation house. It has an open plan of rooms and courtyards, so that wherever you are standing you enjoy a view into a brick-paved courtyard, filled with lime trees, breadfruit and olives or out over the bay toward a coral reef, or into another white walled sparsely furnished room," he wrote. Mrs. Mellon decorated the interiors with understated stylishness: muted colors, wood floors ("warmer and quieter under foot"), painted wicker and rattan furniture, skirted slipcovers, four-poster beds, paintings from their collection, and plants, bulbs, and trees—in soothing

shades of green—in terra-cotta pots. "Bunny's touch is everywhere, and throughout the house there are flowers, from tiny plants in little pots and jars to large informal arrangements," Mr. Mellon wrote.

The main house, adjacent terraces, and guesthouse were on the highest level. Breakfast was served on a terrace under a sheltering arbor. The table was decorated with fresh flowers grouped in white vases. Floating stems of white bougainvillea draped from nearby trees. Chairs and chaises longues with blue cushions were arranged for conversation and for enjoying the view. Bordering the terrace was a low, foot-thick stone wall topped by a wide ledge that served variously as extra seating, a surface for slumbering geckos, and a perch for painting watercolors. The dense surrounding vegetation was sculpted into shapes that best framed the view of the bay below.

The Monkey Room, a drawing room mostly used for entertaining, was furnished with a mix of wicker and rattan pieces in shades of apricot and orange. Paintings, including a Madeline Hewes painting of a monkey, hung on the white walls and sisal rugs lay across painted-wood floors. There were stacks of books and fresh flowers everywhere. "Bunny's quest for comfort and informality have been nurtured with care; a little natural shabbiness in an old chair is sometimes purposely overlooked. The result, I think, is that the [house feels] lived in and loved. More important to me than anything else, [it is] cheerful," Paul Mellon wrote.

In the dining room, a Diego Giacometti chandelier hung over a center table and creamy white panels on the walls opened to reveal storage shelving. The dining room opened into a garden room with a slatted roof, where a collection of myrtle topiaries and clusters of plants—pineapples, white *Portulaca*, white *Vinca*, and hybrid hibiscus—were on display. Small pots of rosemary were placed at random. Across the courtyard in the Ficus Room there were sprays of assorted green and white flowering plants—bougainvillea, begonias, and moonflowers. A female hummingbird built a nest from bits of feathers, leaves, and bark in the branches of a potted citrus. And a chandelier was home to yet another nest. There were plants on side tables, in large circular baskets, and in terra-cotta pots that were painted a creamy white.

A pair of master suites had lovely views of a terrace and a garden resembling George Washington's at Mount Vernon—a pleasure garden featuring flower beds edged with raised stones, around which meandered walkways paved with flagstone laid on the diagonal. Other rooms included a library with views of a reflecting pool and a music room with a grand piano. Throughout the house, overhangs and louvered shutters kept the rooms cool and filtered the harsh rays of the midday sun.

The three-bedroom guesthouse nearby was adorned with floral quilts and bed hangings and boasted panoramic views of the bay. "Because of limited accommodations, guests never number more than three or four," Mr. Mellon wrote. A wine cellar and a swimming pool with a cabana were located a few steps down from the houses, and a path led from the top level down to the beach.

On the middle level were a greenhouse and display gardens. Annual seedlings were potted in the greenhouse,

{ MELLON FAMILY GARDENS }

PAGE 216: The view of the garden terrace and Half Moon Bay from Bunny's bedroom.

PAGE 217: The pristine beach and turquoise waters of crescent-shaped Half Moon Bay.

PAGES 218–19: Steps leading up from the pool terrace to Mr. Mellon's bedroom on the left and the guesthouse on the right.

PAGE 220: A network of walkways and terraces surrounded the house and guesthouse.

PAGE 221, FROM TOP TO BOTTOM: A seating area, featuring one of Bunny's signature geometrically patterned, painted-wood floors; an inviting bedroom for a lucky guest; the airy dining room, illuminated during the day by light filtering in from the garden room to the right and a breezeway, and by a Diego Giacometti chandelier at night.

PAGES 222–23: The garden room, where Bunny displayed favorite plants and trees.

PAGE 223 RIGHT, FROM TOP TO BOTTOM: Plants were propagated in the greenhouse; a blue gate opened from a parking area to a path leading to a reflecting pool by the rose-colored guesthouse; a lattice structure framed the reflecting pool.

OPPOSITE, CLOCKWISE FROM TOP LEFT: Two views of the display, or "hat," gardens on the second level of the property; cabbages growing in the Lower Garden; a nursery of potted trees on the lowest level; an overview of the Lower Garden; plants being propagated in the greenhouse.

TOP RIGHT: A display of myrtle trees in the garden room.

BOTTOM RIGHT: A terrace seating area .

and a nearby shed was converted into a potting station for planting the larger pots. The display gardens, or "hat" gardens, as Lisa Rockwell dubbed them, were raised flower, vegetable, and herb beds surmounted by lattice structures (the "hats") that filtered the sharp rays of the tropical sun.

The lowest level included staff housing, service buildings, and the Lower Garden (a name reminiscent of Mrs. Washington's vegetable garden at Mount Vernon), which was for sowing seeds and propagating flowers and vegetables.

By the summer of 1963, the development of the gardens and landscaping was well underway and a full-time gardener, Charles Post, was in residence. Mrs. Mellon encouraged Post to follow her "trial and error" method of gardening and encouraged him to keep a journal of his work. Expert tree man Everett Hicks was a frequent visitor, and when he was on site, errors were rare. Post wrote in his garden notes that he "densely planted grasses around the beach pump house to hold soil and help screen

the area from the beach until shrubs and trees could be developed," and that "Trees were added to the property from the beach to Mill Reef Road to screen the house from view, and a vegetable garden adjoining the National Park was tilled." Lawn areas were extended and graded, and the existing lawn was fertilized. A "mahogany tree was planted at the guest house," Post noted, and all the trees were trimmed and shaped not only for aesthetics but as "a precaution against storm damage." Post and Hicks roamed the property together, making plans for future planting and development while continuing the practice of trimming hedges and thinning out undesirable trees.

August 1963 was a particularly busy month in the garden. On August 1 an order was placed for ten standard bougainvillea, eighteen crotons, eight hibiscuses, five *Carissa macrocarpa* 'Boxwood Beauty', and two Star Jasmine. The following week brought heavy rains, but the tree planting continued. An avocado was planted in the courtyard, an olive by the parking lot, and Post wrote that he planted "wild rice at the kitchen door and Mahogany trees in the National Park to further screen the hotel from the kitchen area." He noted that the boxwood by the living room window was cut back to "give a better view of the ocean." Later in the month, he wrote that the "lawn in front of the guest house was extended to the pool and planted with grass." Two mahogany trees were planted on the east side, and two thornless acacias were planted near the pool and one by the guesthouse. Toward the end of the month, "an olive and a Bauhinia Purpura were planted at the guest house and an Almond . . . on the beach side of the house," and a white cedar by the beach pump house. "We have scattered seeds and cuttings of all kinds in this area hoping to make it appear as wild as possible" and obscure the view of the house by the time "the season starts," Post wrote. A plan was made for a small orchard near the entrance gate that would include Jamaican ackee, also known as the ackee apple, Fortune and Algerian tangerine, Shaddock and Ruby Red grapefruit, lime and orange trees, sugar apple, and golden apple. A compost pit was dug and leaf mold was collected for use on the potted plants in the shady areas.

The last week of August was "very hot and very dry," Post wrote, but the work continued. He added that they heavily mulched "all the planted material with grass and it was paying dividends in retaining moisture in the ground." The breadfruit was "about seven foot and the loquat looks very good," whereas the mango had a bit of "trouble with scale and while not completely eradicated" was under control. All seemed to be going quite well until wild goats showed up and began chewing up the trees. Precautions were taken, Post wrote, "against further damage." A Cassia fistula and a mahogany tree were planted at the main entrance, he reported, "in an effort to get more color near the house, and a brownea was planted" by the guesthouse, despite a concern about the wind; they weren't sure the plant could stand up to it. The island neighbors were kind. Some lent Post reference books on tropical gardens and others taught him about the growing habits of local plants.

By February 1964, Mr. Hicks had drawn up a grounds maintenance program for four gardeners and their three helpers that included a strong admonition: "All trees are to be preserved at all cost. Do not cut any branches from any trees." This directive came straight from the top—Mrs. Mellon. Not a branch was to be cut, thinned, or pruned without her permission. Ever. Hicks also instructed the gardening staff to keep their tools clean and orderly and stated that "men with assigned helpers are expected to work on the job the same as the helper and are responsible for the performance of duties assigned."

The warm waters and cool breezes off Half Moon Bay made King's Leap an enticing holiday destination for family and friends. Frequent visitors included Jacqueline Kennedy and Hubert de Givenchy. Paul Mellon described a typically bucolic Antigua evening enjoyed with friends:

> Cora will have prepared a delicious meal. Periodic shrieks of laughter emanate from the kitchen as the staff watches "The Jeffersons" on Antiguan television. Dinner is in the candlelit dining room. A huge bowl of tropical fruit serves as a centerpiece on the table, and the warm night air is filled with the sound of tree frogs and the surf breaking gently on the beach a hundred feet below. Merriment is not confined to the kitchen and after dinner the party adjourns to the drawing room for coffee. At this stage I ask solicitously whether anyone would be interested in having a game of Scrabble. The old hands recognize this as a command and draw their chairs up to the table. I take the game seriously, and after I have returned from the bar with drinks, I look suspiciously at the board, pretending to see if there has been any cheating. Finally it is bedtime, and the guests leave me to close the shutters and blow out the candles while they walk under the acacia and black willow trees to their rooms in the nearby guesthouse.

In the early 1970s the Mellons funded a farm collective for the locals in Freetown, a five-mile drive from King's Leap. Mr. Mellon wrote in *Reflections from a Silver Spoon*: "Some years ago Bunny made over a field to the islanders to form a collective, enrich the soil, and grow vegetables for sale to the hotels." The island's main crop, sugarcane, had depleted the soil, making gardening almost impossible. Mrs. Mellon had high expectations for the Freetown

PAGE 226: A courtyard, softly illuminated at night.

TOP LEFT: Hubert de Givenchy sunning himself on the beach at Half Moon Bay.

BOTTOM LEFT: Bunny poses by an allegedly poisonous tree.

OPPOSITE: The two friends relaxing on a terrace.

PAGE 230: Bunny shopping for fruit at a local market.

Garden, as she called it, writing, "The purpose of the Gardening Program is to create work—to instruct in the use of knowledge of growing vegetables and fruits. The importance in the care of the land as a year's sound source of income—that men can till the soil—make an income—and be fed. I hope that the investment of hope and the financial boost to start it off will bring something to this island that they can call their own and trust the white man from outside." But the venture failed. The poor soil and the islanders' lack of interest, Paul Mellon wrote, "defeated Bunny's plans, and the field has reverted to scrubland, an over-grown memorial to a noble enterprise." Mrs. Mellon was ahead of her time; today the tradition of backyard gardening has been restored. She also worked to establish medical facilities to provide health care for the Antiguans, as Paul Mellon noted in his autobiography, "So Bunny has now, with professional medical advice, equipped a laboratory and clinic fully staffed by trained men and women mostly from the islands."

In 1974 the garden plan was expanded to include the propagation of hibiscus in the greenhouse and a substantial increase in vegetable production. Hibiscus cuttings were taken at Longwood Gardens in Pennsylvania and shipped to the island in March. Later in the year, many varieties of vegetable seeds were delivered: cabbage (Jersey Wakefield and Emerald Cross); carrot (Touchon, Gold Pak, and Short and Sweet); cucumber (Marketer, Ashley, and Victory); beet (Detroit Dark Red and Perfected Detroit Dark Red); bean (Tendergreen Bush and Lima Fordhook 242, for sandwiches); leek (Elephant and American Flag); watermelon (Congo and Dixie Queen); tomato (Rutgers, Hawaiian Tropic, and Red Currant); radish (Red Boy and Early Scarlet Globe); and lettuce (Bibb, Matchless, May King, Great Lakes, Butter King, Oak Leaf, and White Boston). Seeds for white flowers—*Alyssum* 'Carpet of Snow', dusty miller, and Impatiens Baby White—were also delivered.

Plants sent from the Oak Spring greenhouse included three geraniums; three *Allium* (*sphaerocephalon*, *schubertii*, and *carinatum pulchellum*); three *Dianthus*; four *Nicotiana alata* 'Lime Green'; two miniature white *Nicotiana alata*; one myrtle tree; two *Senecio cineraria*, or dusty miller; three annual mums; six ferns; one Pyrethrum gray foliage; one anemone blue; two *Catananche caerulea*; three orchids (*Sophronitis grandiflora*, *Brassavola perrinii*, and blue *Brassavola cordata*); and two amaryllis.

Long-distance gardening demanded accurate record keeping, and Everett Hicks instructed the gardeners to record the following:

Soil amendment—what and how much was added.
Fertilizer—rates and amounts.
Pesticides applied—rates, crops applied to, number of
*   gallons, and results.*
Disease problems and solutions used.

"Soil samples are to be taken once or twice a year," Hicks wrote, and "observations and cultural information should be noted on the various crops."

In the early 1990s Mrs. Mellon ordered twenty-three varieties of roses for Antigua, including Graham Thomas, Sir Walter Raleigh, Dainty Bess, Queen Elizabeth, and Angel Face from Wayside Roses, and Sheer Bliss, Graceland, Blue Ribbon, Pristine, First Kiss, Class Act, and Summer Fashion from Jackson & Perkins.

By the 1993 season, structures had begun to show wear and tear and were in need of repair. Tomato and pepper cages were rebuilt, as were a compost bin, a tool-storage shed, and a seedling shed. The lattice of the "hat" gardens was also showing signs of disrepair, and Mrs. Mellon planned for a redo.

Other envisioned changes to the property included converting the lawn by the pool from Bermuda grass to Cashmere Zoysia grass, adding tangerines from Barbados to the guesthouse entrance, and planting Mrs. Mellon's favored varieties of petunias in her private bedroom garden. For the terrace off the dining room she planned to add a nutmeg tree, *Thunbergia*, New Guinea impatiens, white bougainvillea, and passion fruit. Around the pool she wanted to plant white hibiscus, a miniature peach oleander and one large white oleander. And she wanted a few lavender *Vanda* or *Dendrobium* orchids to place around the house, as well as a few miniature orchids growing on bark.

It was of great importance to Bunny for all the plants to be correctly labeled and for the hanging baskets to be regularly freshened. As for trees, she wanted some banana trees planted near the house where they could easily be viewed, as well as Persian lime, Meyer lemon, nutmeg, 'Lula' avocado, and the pink Barbados variety of paw paw. In time, all the planning and hard work began to pay off, as Mr. Mellon noticed, "The gardens have grown to maturity and brought the whole place to perfection." Indeed.

Every year the winter season ended all too soon, it seemed, and it was wheels up for the Gulfstream—its shiny nose pointed toward Virginia. Springtime had arrived at the farm.

Kennedy Family Gardens

ROSE GARDEN, WHITE HOUSE

It began at the Palace of Versailles in June 1961, when John F. Kennedy was visiting France for the first time as president of the United States. The French president, Charles de Gaulle, hosted the Kennedys at a glittering dinner in the Hall of Mirrors, followed by a ballet performance at the château's Royal Opera House. The grand finale was an unhurried, silent drive through the royal gardens in the dark of night. Hugh Sidey, a journalist traveling with the president, recorded that drive for posterity:

After the performance, the Kennedys, with their hosts, slowly motored through the grounds and the gardens of Versailles. The mist still clung, giving the vast cobblestoned courtyards the mystery and romance that they had held for the French rulers who once lived there. Huge spotlights bathed the buildings in diffused beams. The fountains glowed and sparkled, the shadows of the statues reaching into the black and conjuring up the heritage of grandeur. Twice, the Kennedys stopped to gaze on this haunting scene. And the last time, the President took the arm of his wife as they walked over the damp lawn, silent, deeply moved. President de Gaulle joined them and the two Presidents solemnly shook hands and said good night.

President de Gaulle used the majestic grounds surrounding the Palace of Versailles to advantage. JFK noticed and began to think that the right kind of garden at the White House could be useful to advance his New Frontier ideas and programs—and simultaneously position the United States in a positive light on the world stage.

A few months later, while vacationing on Cape Cod, President Kennedy sailed with his family to the Mellons' beachfront home in Osterville on Nantucket Sound for an afternoon picnic. (The menu most likely included Mellon family favorites: corn on the cob, fried chicken, vegetable salad, blueberry pie, and vanilla ice cream.) Mrs. Mellon recalled the afternoon in an article titled "President Kennedy's Garden": "My involvement began at a picnic on a hazy summer day in August at our beach house on Cape Cod, surrounded by sand dunes, the sea, and sailboats. . . . Hardly had the President come ashore from his boat when he suggested we sit down and discuss a garden for the White House." The president did indeed get right to the point, telling her that the White House had no garden equal in quality or attractiveness to the gardens he had seen and in which he had been entertained in Europe. He wanted an American garden, open and expansive, designed for function and beauty in the traditions established by two of America's founding fathers—Washington and Jefferson. His wish list included a lawn large enough to hold a thousand people with a continuous display of colorful flowers and a new set of steps to connect his office to the garden. Even though Mrs. Mellon considered herself an amateur, she couldn't resist such an exciting assignment and agreed to give it some thought.

On a hot, humid day in September she brought her friend the landscape architect Perry Wheeler to the White House to assess the proposed site. As they sat in the shade of Andrew Jackson's tall *Magnolia grandiflora*, they were surprised to see President Kennedy walking briskly toward them, grinning and full of questions about the garden. She recounted their conversation in her article: "'What do you think can be done? Have you any ideas?' Although I had no thoughts of what to do at the moment, the President's enthusiasm and interest were so contagious that I felt I must certainly find him a good solution." She and

Mr. Wheeler found the setting stark and unfriendly, surrounded by white buildings and ornamented with only a few white, straggly 'Tom Thumb' roses. "It was an interesting problem involving a fascinating place."

The Rose Garden is bordered by the West Wing building to the west, a long colonnade to the north, and the residence to the east. To the south, the garden is open to a sweeping view of the South Lawn. The space has been reinvented many times over the last two hundred years, beginning with the small buildings that Thomas Jefferson built on either side of the mansion. These service buildings, the original west and east wings, were similar to those he had built at Monticello. Each extended one hundred feet, was fronted by a long, covered walkway, and was divided into offices and storage rooms. The west wing included a room for ice, another for firewood (with coal storage below), and a servant's privy, or necessary room.

In the mid-nineteenth century, the space gradually became filled with greenhouses and a large conservatory bursting with roses, orchids, camellias, palm trees, and potted fruit trees, which were favorites of Ulysses Grant. When Teddy Roosevelt tore down the greenhouses and conservatory to make way for a new office building, later called the West Wing, his wife Edith shed a few tears but soon had the vacant rectangular space converted into a formal, parterre-style Colonial garden, featuring beds of roses and old-fashioned flowers in a swirling geometric design. Ellen Wilson supplanted Mrs. Roosevelt's garden with a strict plan of hedges and beds of roses that ran in straight lines on either side of a central lawn and a formal president's walk lined with standard roses that ran parallel to the colonnade. For the first time it was called a rose garden. Franklin Roosevelt enlisted the services of Frederick Law Olmsted Jr. to develop a comprehensive landscape plan for the White House grounds that is still in use today and is known as the "Bible." Olmsted told FDR that the formal gardens on the east and west sides of the mansion were the intimate and private areas of the landscape and that the flower plantings should be confined to these two gardens. During the Truman administration, the interior of the crumbling old residence was gutted and refitted

PAGES 232–33: The Rose Garden, looking west toward the Cabinet Room in the West Wing.

PAGE 234: Katherine crab apple trees and tulips border the colonnade on the north side of the Rose Garden.

PAGE 235: Tulips open to the midday sun in the Rose Garden.

ABOVE: During lunch at the Mellon family beach house on Cape Cod in the summer of 1961, JFK asked Bunny to redesign the Rose Garden.

PAGE 238 TOP: Bunny's hand-drawn plan for the Rose Garden.

PAGE 238 BOTTOM: Bunny's watercolor of the Rose Garden. The president approved all of her ideas for its redesign, except for the tent.

PAGE 239: The northern and southern floral borders, corner magnolia trees, and the redesigned steps that JFK requested are all visible in this aerial view.

PAGE 240: President Kennedy granted honorary citizenship to Winston Churchill on the redesigned Rose Garden steps. Churchill's son, Randolph (standing to the president's left), accepted on his father's behalf.

PAGE 242 LEFT: Mrs. Mellon conferring with one of the "G men," as she called them, as the magnolia trees were being planted in the Rose Garden.

PAGE 242 RIGHT: It took a large crew to carefully set the *Magnolia* x *soulangeana* in the four corners of the Rose Garden.

PAGE 243: President Kennedy enjoyed a clear view of this magnolia from his desk in the Oval Office.

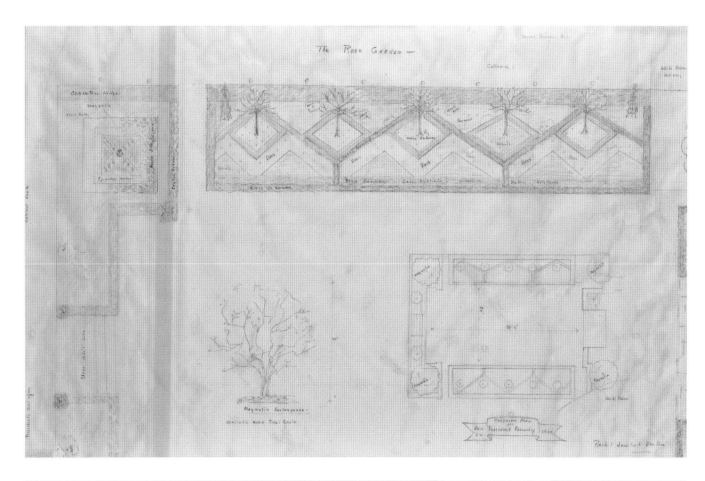

with steel beams. Amid all the renovations, the Trumans managed to plant a few white roses that soldiered on in the garden—the "pitiful little Tom Thumb roses" that Mrs. Mellon had seen that memorable afternoon.

Some time passed before she finally found a starting point for the design of the garden. One cold October evening, on a routine walk near her Manhattan townhouse, she noticed the bare magnolia trees in front of the Frick Collection, trees she had long admired, but on this particular evening it was as if she were seeing them for the first time. She was struck by the beauty of their shape as the light filtered through their branches. As she recounted in her article, she had "hoped to find an inspiration that would help me bring all of the President's requirements together," and she thought that magnolias would soften the white structures and anchor the garden in the four corners, especially the tricky northeast corner, where the colonnade abutted the much taller residence. They would also allow light to pass through for plantings underneath, creating a lovely garden atmosphere. "Their pale, silvery branches with heavy twigs seemed to retain the light of

summer. I knew their pattern of growth would continue to give form in winter and would catch raindrops as well as tufts of falling snow. I felt I could now design the President's garden!"

Finally on January 27, 1962, she penned a note to the president on her light blue stationery:

Dear Mr. President,

 This is my suggestion as a design for your garden.

 The flowers will be changed with the season.

 The tent at the end will be put up in summer and removed in winter.

 This would give a place to sit and dine out doors yet with protection.

 All the details have been discussed with the Park Service Department. They have most of the plant material available and can start work at any time.

 If this is not near the idea you had in mind please don't hesitate to tell me and I will begin again.

   Sincerely,

   Bunny Mellon

Two days later the President said no to the tent and yes to the rest. A crew from the National Park Service would provide the labor.

She began to sketch her ideas, creating a skeleton drawing—the bones of the garden—taking into account, as she always did when starting a design, climate, exposure to sunlight, the dimensions of the space, and how much time could be given to maintenance when it was finished.

The four magnolias anchoring the four corners gave structure to the plan. Bunny designed two intricate, 12-foot-wide beds to border the north and south sides of the lawn. Each bed would be punctuated with five diamond-shaped sections edged with santolina. In the center of each diamond, a *Malus* 'Katherine' (Katherine crab apple) would be planted. She chose Katherines for the shade they offer in the heat of summer, their handsome form in winter, and the profusion of delicate, peachy

pink flowers they produce for two or three weeks every spring. To frame the garden, she selected a variety of boxwood shrubs, including *Buxus* 'Kingsville' (Kingsville boxwood) and three different sizes of *Buxus sempervirens* 'Suffruticosa' (dwarf English boxwood). The shrubs were to be planted along the length of the beds, at the corners of the lawn, and in a zigzag pattern through the diamond-shaped sections. An *Osmanthus ilicifolius* (holly osmanthus) hedge would border the president's covered walkway along the northern boundary.

As the president had requested, the steps leading from his office portico into the garden were redesigned to his specifications. He wanted the central step to be larger and wider than the others so that it could serve as a platform for presentations and speeches. And he wanted the three steps above it to be where honorees would stand, so that he would not be positioned above them. He was also keenly interested in the floral program and put in a special request for plants named in Thomas Jefferson's garden journals, which he had read.

To keep the president's beloved lawn in tiptop shape, it was sodded with Merion bluegrass. In later years, a mixture of Kentucky bluegrass and creeping red fescue, a combination of southern and northern grasses, were sprinkled in with the Merion to mitigate the troublesome effects of Washington, D.C.'s swampy climate on the lawn. Limited air circulation in the confined garden, combined with a maintenance program that includes frequent watering, creates an environment for mildew and fungi.

Every garden needs a gardener, and though there were gardeners on staff at the White House, none was assigned specifically to the project. Mrs. Kennedy asked Mrs. Mellon to go and find a gardener. Irvin Williams recalled his first encounter with her, "I was told the First Lady and Mrs. Paul Mellon are coming to talk to you. When the car came around, it was just Mrs. Mellon. It was a great meeting; we discussed her plans and her commitment to the president's garden. She said she would appreciate it if I could assist her. We talked about the plant material needed. I told her I'd been in conversation with Park Service officials about what was happening down around the Tidal Basin and explained that the Park Service was running a sewer line through the pansy garden and the large magnolias nearby would have to go—be moved or destroyed—to accommodate the new line, and she wanted to see them right away."

That very day, Mr. Williams and Mrs. Mellon forged what she later referred to as a "meeting of minds" and a "perfect rapport." And they remained dear friends for the rest of Mrs. Mellon's life. Two days after their first meeting they located a group of *Magnolia* x *soulangeana* (saucer magnolias) near Hains Point in East Potomac Park on the Potomac River, three of which had the airy, slender form she was looking for. They tagged them for the garden and found one more at the DC War Memorial in West Potomac Park. Growing in crowded conditions, it had developed an unusual shape—a flat back and uncommon height from reaching for the light—just right for that odd northeast corner.

Finding the trees was one thing; getting them installed was another matter entirely. On March 8, 1962, Perry Wheeler wrote to Mrs. Mellon, who was in Antigua at the time. "Dear Bunny, How I wish you could have been at the [Department of the] Interior Building yesterday when I went down to meet with the Park Department boys about plans for the garden."

The National Park Service had informed Mr. Wheeler that Mrs. Mellon's plan to plant magnolias, or any trees for that matter, in the garden had to be abandoned because of the great number of cables running beneath the soil. Mr. Wheeler explained that if there couldn't be any trees, Mrs. Mellon would have to redesign the garden. This threw the "boys" into a state of shock. Everything—plants, soil, and equipment—had been ordered and scheduled, and the Park Service could not imagine changing a thing at that late date, with the exception, of course, of forgoing the trees. "It did not seem to enter their heads what not having the trees would do to your plan," Mr. Wheeler added.

The boys pressed on. They insisted that it would be extremely difficult to plant the two trees by the Oval Office because of the slope. And they volunteered their personal critique of the tallest tree, "This 'cucumber magnolia' grows much too large and the flowers are not very good."

Mr. Wheeler suggested a solution: plant them in large, hidden boxes. He told Mrs. Mellon that he also "tried to explain that I thought you were much more interested in the form, shape and winter character, etc., of the trees than you were in the flowers, since they last such a short time."

In truth, the Park Service crew had decided that the trees would be too costly to move and preferred to buy cheaper trees in a nursery. Perry Wheeler wrote to Mrs. Mellon that Irvin Williams was tapped to handle the situation because "he seemed to understand the problem and knew more about the effect she wanted than anyone else." In the end, Mr. Williams conducted a stealth operation. With as little fuss as possible, he had the trees transferred from East and West Potomac Parks to the White House in the dead of night.

And the boys acquiesced, admitting that all four trees could be planted, including the one with the flat back, which could, in fact, "be gotten in close to the corner of the house"—exactly what Mrs. Mellon had wanted all along.

They dug a test hole around the buried cables and proceeded as planned. Then Perry Wheeler decided it would be a good idea to mark out the design. At first the boys objected, but soon realized that it made sense and agreed to have it done before Mrs. Mellon returned to D.C.

The Department of the Interior issued an official statement announcing the commencement of the project: "Region Six of the National Park Service began redevelopment of the West Rose Garden on March 19th. This project, which is being carried out by Park Service personnel with the approval of the Director, National Park Service, involves use of available plant materials from the Park Service's Daingerfield Island nurseries." In closing, the statement read," Mrs. Paul Mellon, a member of the Fine Arts Committee for the White House, has served as a special advisor to the Park Service on the design of the West Rose Garden."

Finally, the work could begin. Mrs. Mellon and Mrs. Kennedy met on the South Portico with Irvin Williams, Perry Wheeler, and J. B. West, chief usher of the White House, for a private ribbon cutting of sorts and a blessing of the garden, probably the only formal meeting they ever had. Mrs. Kennedy embraced the moment, talked about the president's "beloved garden" and about how he had learned to appreciate gardens while traveling in France, Austria, and England.

On Friday, March 30, the dormant magnolias were brought from a greenhouse and set in the four corners of the garden by tree expert Everett Hicks under Mrs. Mellon's exacting eye. A backhoe loader leveled the soil at the base of the trees to grade and a ditch was dug for the irrigation drain.

As the work began, Mrs. Mellon recalled, "Mr. Williams and I realized the garden needed to be wider than the plan called for; the proportion wasn't quite right. So we asked the 'G men' [National Park Service crew] to move the measuring string on the south boundary over another eighteen inches. Without any discussion or even a moment of thought, they said 'No,' turned away and went back to work. Well, Mr. Williams and I decided we'd wait. As soon as they left for lunch, Mr. Williams quietly went over, measured the additional eighteen inches, and moved the string! When the crew returned from lunch, they didn't notice a thing, or if they did, they said not a word but went straight to work. We got our way," she added, "the Irv Williams way."

At 11:28 A.M. on Saturday, March 31, the president's schedule was unceremoniously interrupted by an off-the-

record meeting with Major General Chester V. Clifton. Mrs. Mellon's "hoe" had sliced through an unknown buried cable—the hot line that set off the nation's military alert. The secrecy around the incident caused a frenzy, and the *New York Times* sent their reporters scrambling for a lead. On April 2 the *Times* reported, "An atomic war alert ended in seconds. Faulty alert sent planes to runway." The president later privately joked that now they finally knew where that cable was, and the work continued.

During the first weeks of April the irrigation system was installed and the Katherine crab apples were planted. The next step was to dig up the central portion of the garden to a depth of four feet and fill it with rich planting soil. A backhoe loader leveled the soil to grade and the lawn was tilled and sodded. The osmanthus hedge was planted along the colonnade to enclose the president's walkway, and the steps were framed. Dwarf boxwood was set along the edges of the lawn and in the two parallel flower beds in its zigzag pattern. The president kept a close and watchful eye as the beds were planted with flowers.

On April 24 the garden was officially finished, but everyone kept working. Mr. Williams said they wanted the garden "to be as lovely as it could be." And for him, that

would be for another forty-six years. Though everything seemed to proceed smoothly, there were some aggravations. Mrs. Mellon had her share of meddlers in the form of unwanted trees and plants that mysteriously appeared overnight. To address the situation, Mrs. Kennedy wrote a letter to Captain Tazewell T. Shepard, Naval Aide to the President, that read, "I would appreciate it if the entire care and planning of the grounds would be left completely to Mr. Williams. I do not think he needs any advice as the plans Mrs. Mellon and he have formed could not be improved upon." That seemed to halt the incursion of interlopers.

In the 1960s, greenhouse space at the White House was nonexistent (there is little more today), and to meet the need for dedicated space to support the garden's floral displays, Mrs. Mellon found an area adjacent to the nearby Kenilworth Aquatic Gardens (where Mr. Williams had worked as chief horticulturist) large enough for several greenhouses. But when the bids for the greenhouse contract came in, Mrs. Mellon's favored greenhouse company, Lord & Burnham, was not the lowest bidder. This may be a non-issue in the private sector, but it presents a formidable hurdle in the government sector. Once again, Mrs. Kennedy stepped in and dealt swiftly with the matter, writing to Conrad Wirth, director of the National Park Service, on November 30, 1962: "Mrs. Mellon is the member of my Fine Arts Committee who is the advisor on all gardens, plantings, etc. here. Could you do me an enormous favor and discuss the present situation with her? What I would hope is this. . . the contract was only signed for one greenhouse—can we get that one finished and, then, switch to Lord and Burnham?" According to Mr. Williams, the greenhouses, or "potting structures," as he called them, were built by Lord & Burnham—in his opinion the "Cadillac" of greenhouses.

When the garden was completed, President Kennedy wanted "the world" to see it and used it as the backdrop for important events. On April 9, 1963, for instance, he presided with relish and fanfare over the bestowing of honorary United States citizenship on Sir Winston Churchill, whom he called, "a son of America." Former White House curator Jim Ketchum recorded his recollections of the event:

After Mrs. Mellon finished overseeing her redesign of the Rose Garden in 1962, not only was the area a great favorite of JFK's, but he soon scheduled ceremonies, announcements, etc. for the space. The Churchill citizenship ceremony was held in late morning on a sunny spring day with tulips in full bloom and flowering ornamentals adding frosting to the cake. The garden was very crowded with standees spilling over onto the walkway that connected the Mansion to the West Wing. I remember looking out from the walkway as President Kennedy introduced Randolph Churchill, who was accepting the honor on behalf of his father. Undoubtedly, JFK's love of the Garden and its potential as a stage for ceremonial events, coupled with the colorful beds of spring flowers, made it a natural setting for the Churchill ceremony.

Congresswoman Lindy Boggs recalled her moment with President Kennedy in the Rose Garden: "We went out to the little garden. He remarked on what a restful, lovely respite from his thinking and his duties that garden had become for him. And he said, 'The chrysanthemums have been so beautiful. Lindy, how long do chrysanthe-mums stay in bloom?' He was reluctant to have them go away. And I said, 'Well, until the frost comes, usually.'"

The bounty of the garden served an unexpected and bittersweet purpose following that fateful November day. For President Kennedy's funeral services, Mrs. Mellon worked with the White House florists to create floral arrangements for the East Room of the White House, the Rotunda in the U.S. Capitol, and Cathedral of St. Matthew, and for his grave she filled a willow basket with cuttings from the garden. For all the years that he worked at the White House, Irvin Williams continued this practice on the anniversary of the president's death. He filled a small basket with flowers from the Rose Garden, took it to Arlington Cemetery, and laid it on the president's grave.

Senator Robert F. Kennedy revealed the impact that the garden had on his brother when he wrote, "Mrs. Mellon had made everything cheerful and pleasant," and he told her, "President Kennedy spent more time worrying about the Rose Garden and how the two of you were going to handle it than he did about the Cuban Missile Crisis or Berlin."

It became clear that Mrs. Mellon's Rose Garden would stand the test of time when Lady Bird Johnson recorded her first guided tour as First Lady in her diary: "I pointed out

President Kennedy's magnolia soulangeana, the gaillardia, or Indian blanket that grows in masses wild in Texas in the spring, the gloriosa daisies which are a fabulous flash of color in all four corners of the garden this summer, the white roses for which the garden is named but which really are very few in number, and the lovely asters."

Twenty years later Mrs. Mellon was still getting calls from the White House. In an exchange with Nancy Reagan on June 14, 1981, they discussed the aging Katherine crab apples. Mrs. Reagan asked her what could be done about them. Mrs. Mellon wrote back, "I am sorry to have taken so long to replace the Rose Garden. . . . Perhaps we should take advantage of the age and feeling of the old crab apples, rather than replant the garden as it was twenty years ago . . . remove the large cumbersome front hedge and put in a lower, more delicate one. . . . The two hollies in front of the President's office should be removed. This Mr. Williams will do as soon as possible to let in light."

And, as she was always thinking about ways to improve the garden, she added, "In fall we will make a new planting plan—very little can grow with the apple tree shade and roots. . . . I would like to change it a little in feeling, adding more gray plants and a few older white roses—with lovely lilies that would be blooming in June. It was so kind of you to ask me to redo it—and I hope that the great interest that President Kennedy had to create it will go another step forward in continuing it with President Reagan. I will do my best to add or subtract ideas that have occurred during the long interval. Having talked to you and meeting the President the other day, one wants it to be the best ever."

Since that time, Irvin Williams says, the Katherine crab apples "grew so well that they ended up shading the flower display." The canopy of shade they created made it necessary to restage the garden to maximize "the show"—the seasonal floral display. The roses were moved to the front

of the beds, to "reach the sun and for effect." The gardeners began to put the plants in pots so they could quickly be exchanged for fresher ones. And in 2007 the old crab apples were finally replaced. The new ones were transplanted from the sandy soil of New Jersey and initially struggled to generate fibrous roots. They flowered only a little the first year, but by the third year they were thriving.

When Mrs. Mellon was encouraged to redraw her Rose Garden design for posterity's sake, she did it reluctantly. "It is a bore to go back and redo something. . . . All I really care about is that it turns out well. Then I can turn to the next." As she was fond of saying, "There is not too much that can be said about a garden. Its greatest reality is not a reality, for a garden, hovering always in a state of becoming, sums up its own past and its future."

249

PAGE 244: Kennedy performed a "happy duty" when he conferred American citizenship on Sir Winston Churchill on April 9, 1963, in the Rose Garden.

PAGE 245 LEFT: John F. Kennedy Jr. in his father's garden.

PAGE 245 RIGHT: Caroline Kennedy riding her pony, Macaroni, on the South Lawn while her father's new garden was under construction.

PAGE 246 LEFT: The president and his young son share a quiet moment on the colonnade outside the Oval Office.

PAGE 246 RIGHT: President Kennedy conferring with his brother Robert on the colonnade outside the Oval Office before Bunny's redesign of the Rose Garden.

PAGE 247, CLOCKWISE FROM TOP LEFT: Tulips in full bloom; each of the ten crab apple trees in the beds bordering the lawn was underplanted with seasonal flowers and a diamond-shaped border of santolina; the north flower bed in autumn, looking toward the West Wing; yellow tulips brighten the flower beds in spring; the intricate pattern Bunny designed for the beds bordering the lawn is clearly visible from this vantage point; President Kennedy requested a lawn large enough to hold a thousand people.

PAGES 248–49: The crab apple trees in full bloom.

PAGE 249 RIGHT: The crab apple trees just about to bloom.

OPPOSITE: The bed on the south side of the Rose Garden with the Old Executive Office Building in the background.

ABOVE: The bed on the north side of the lawn in the fall.

JACQUELINE KENNEDY GARDEN, WHITE HOUSE

President Kennedy, delighted with the new Rose Garden, began to make plans for the next garden project—a redesign of the East Garden on the opposite side of the White House. Once again, he reached out to Mrs. Mellon. She later wrote, "At the time there was no garden for the First Lady, her children and their friends, so they [the Kennedys] decided this would be the main purpose." Irvin Williams confirmed that it was a garden intended for Mrs. Kennedy and future first ladies. Mrs. Mellon, whose advice about garden design was to "take special care about what you want," sketched out a preliminary plan with Mrs. Kennedy, including a terrace for lunches and tea, a place where children could pick flowers, a small pool with a splashing fountain, a lawn for children's games, and herb beds for the kitchen. And, keeping in mind Mrs. Kennedy's restoration of the interior of the White House, Mrs. Mellon wrote in her journal that the "quality of the interior had to be matched in the garden." It "ought to . . . correspond to the place and environment. It should inspire, calm and always have a feeling people could take home—even copy." Then tragedy struck—and everything changed.

The eastern grounds of the White House, now the first view of presidential life visitors have as they begin a tour of the White House, have undergone many changes over the years. In Jefferson's day the expanse was bordered by the residence to the west and the colonnade he had constructed to the north, which fronted an attached service building that initially served as an ice house and wine cellar and later as a storage space for garden tools and other equipment. In 1866 the colonnade and service building were removed to make way for an elaborate secondary entrance on the east façade of the residence. By 1902, Theodore Roosevelt had added the East Wing office building and rebuilt Jefferson's colonnade and service building, which included a cloakroom and was later converted into a movie theater. His wife Edith created a formal parterre garden featuring paths that circled flower beds filled with ornamental, old-fashioned flowers that bloomed through the seasons: black-eyed Susans, hollyhocks, tulips, roses, and asters. This new garden complemented her Colonial garden on the west side.

A decade later, Ellen Wilson worked with noted landscape designer Beatrix Farrand on a plan for a new formal design, the central focus of which was a reflecting pool. Mrs. Wilson's premature death halted all progress; Wilson's second wife, Edith, wholeheartedly embraced the plan and authorized Mrs. Farrand to plant the garden according to Ellen's wishes. In a bittersweet twist of fate, Woodrow Wilson spent many afternoons in the garden convalescing from his stroke. In the late 1940s, Harry and Bess Truman replaced the Wilsons' reflecting pool with a wide expanse of grass and planted Tom Thumb roses.

After Kennedy's death, as the nation was coming to grips with the devastating loss, the East Garden's most poignant transformation was begun. On Friday, March 20, 1964, Lady Bird Johnson wrote in *A White House Diary*:

This morning I had an appointment that I have been looking forward to very much. Mrs. Paul Mellon came at 10:30 to walk around the gardens with me. She is one of the great authorities on gardens, on planting in general, and a working-at-it authority, a planning, creative authority. It was she who

implemented the things Mrs. Kennedy wanted to get done on the White House grounds, transforming the Rose Garden into a thing of exquisite beauty.

I was anxious to meet her because I want excellence to be applauded and preserved. We reviewed lovingly every detail of the story of the Rose Garden, walked around most of the grounds, and then went into a similar garden on the east side. Mrs. Mellon has a plan to transform it into a very dainty, feminine garden and put up a little plaque as a tribute to Jacqueline Kennedy for all she did for the White House.

Soon thereafter, work on the garden began. The same team that had worked with Mrs. Mellon on the Rose Garden was assembled: Everett Hicks, Perry Wheeler, Irvin Williams, and J. B. West. The National Park Service again provided the labor.

At that time, the structure beneath the East Garden—a bomb shelter—had been under renovation, and all the plant material had been temporarily moved to A. Gude Sons, a nursery in Rockville, Maryland. The plants didn't survive, however, and the White House was offered replacements. As Mr. Williams recalled, "It was a blessing that the other plant material didn't make it. We got top-choice replacements, and they were donated at no extra cost. That removed the restrictions on the replanting."

The inspiration for the overall design of the garden arose when Mrs. Kennedy mentioned to Mrs. Mellon that she'd like to have a croquet court for her children. This comment sparked Mrs. Mellon's imagination, bringing to mind *Alice in Wonderland*, "particularly the game of make-believe with playing cards as gardeners, standing among the standard rosebushes," Mrs. Mellon wrote in an article titled "The Jacqueline Kennedy Garden." "A few weeks before I had seen topiary holly trees in A. Gude's Nursery in Rockville, Maryland, with marvelous high chess like shapes made of clipped American holly." From there the idea came to life and everything fell into place.

The East Garden was the same length as the Rose Garden but twenty inches narrower (for some reason, Mrs. Mellon didn't add the extra inches to this garden as

she had to the Rose Garden). Echoing the layout of the Rose Garden, a central lawn was flanked by two beds to the north and south, each planted with five topiary hollies. Each of the trees was surrounded by a square bed planted with herbs for the kitchen—thyme, chives, basil, dill, sage, and parsley—as well as flowers for little hands to pick, including marigolds, nasturtiums, pansies, and Queen Anne's lace. Low hedges of Kingsville boxwood bordered the beds, and a grass path, bordered by the Kingsville boxwood hedge on one side and a *Buxus sempervirens* hedge on the other ran the length of the northern bed.

Gracing the east end was a shallow, rectangular pool, overlooked by a bronze sculpture, Sylvia Shaw Judson's *The Little Gardener*, a gift from Mrs. Mellon. On November 18, 1964, Perry Wheeler wrote to New York architect H. Page Cross asking him to "send a plan for the trellis that is to go at the back of the pergola in the East Garden. Mr. Williams has some carpenters who are free to build it now." This painted-wood pergola was constructed at the west end. It was planted with Concord grapes and adorned with hanging baskets. As Mrs. Mellon wrote in "The Jacqueline Kennedy Garden," the baskets were filled with "scented geraniums and tubs of lemon verbena, heliotrope and mignonette." By the 1980s, lattice windows that opened onto a view across the south grounds toward the Washington Monument had been added to three sides of the pergola. Hawthorn, hollies, *Magnolia* x *soulangeana*, lilacs, and flowering crab apple trees dotted

the surrounding area. A pea gravel path punctuated with garden benches ringed the perimeter of the garden. As in the Rose Garden, an osmanthus hedge was planted along the southern boundary.

On the northern boundary, the historic colonnade had been enclosed with windows, and the walkway had become unbearably warm in the summer. Mrs. Mellon's solution was to plant eight linden trees, one per pillar, in front of the colonnade. The lindens were kept pruned to a height of eight feet for visibility, and their foliage shaded the walkway. In addition, as Irvin Williams recalled, there was "a border of flowers under the lindens [weaving] in and out to create a pattern that flowed." The flowers included tulips and *Fritillaria imperialis* (Crown imperial) in the spring and *Santolina chamaecyparissus* (lavender cotton) and *Hosta sieboldiana* 'Elegans' (plaintain lily) in the summer. As President Kennedy had requested, two large *Magnolia* x *soulangeana* 'Alexandrina' trees were planted at the northwest and southeast corners.

It was Mrs. Johnson's idea to rename the garden the "Jacqueline Kennedy Garden," although Mrs. Kennedy didn't want her to. Even Congress overruled her. Mrs. Kennedy felt that the living memorial should be in honor

of, and credited to, her husband. She also rejected the idea of a permanent plaque, agreeing only to have her name "scratched on the back of a bench." Nevertheless, a plaque, written in Mrs. Mellon's hand, was attached to one of the pergola's columns. It reads, "This garden is dedicated to Jacqueline Kennedy with great affection by those who worked with her in the White House."

An emotional dedication ceremony was held in the garden at 2:00 P.M. on Thursday, April 22, 1965. Bess Abell, Mrs. Johnson's social secretary, recalled that Mrs. Johnson had hoped that Mrs. Kennedy would attend, but she was represented by her mother, Janet Auchincloss, instead. Mr. and Mrs. Mellon were there, as were Senator Robert Kennedy and his wife, Ethel. Mrs. Johnson acknowledged Mrs. Kennedy's contributions to improving the White House, saying, "I dedicate it to the enduring heritage she has given all of us."

Lady Bird Johnson added a personal note in her diary, "Mrs. Mellon is an easy, unassuming person; I like her very much. And although I could by no means match knowledge with knowledge, I can at least match it with understanding and appreciation and let her know how much it means to thousands of people."

PAGE 252: The pergola at the west end of the Jacqueline Kennedy Garden.

PAGE 253: The dedication plaque, dated April 22, 1965.

PAGE 255: The flower bed on the south side of the Jacqueline Kennedy Garden.

PAGE 256 LEFT: Bunny's gift to the garden was this statue, *The Little Gardener*, by Sylvia Shaw Judson. It overlooks the pool at the east end of the garden.

PAGES 256–57: The lattice "windows" that were added to the pergola in the 1980s open to views of the South Lawn.

OPPOSITE: *Alice's Adventures in Wonderland* was the inspiration for the topiary hollies punctuating the north bed.

ABOVE LEFT: Bunny with Robert F. Kennedy at the garden dedication ceremony.

ABOVE RIGHT: Lady Bird Johnson with Janet Auchincloss, Jacqueline Kennedy's mother, who stood in for her at the dedication ceremony.

RIGHT: The site of the dedication ceremony in the newly renamed Jacqueline Kennedy Garden.

JOHN F. KENNEDY GRAVE SITE

As the shocking news of President Kennedy's assassination on Friday, November 22, 1963, circled the globe, those closest to him—his family, friends, and the staff members who had toiled by his side—had to channel their disbelief and grief into planning a funeral and arranging a burial. Initial media reports announced that the president's body would be buried near his infant son's in their home state of Massachusetts, but everything changed when his widow declared that the president "belonged to the people." • On Saturday, November 23, the slain president's brother Attorney General Robert F. Kennedy and Secretary of Defense Robert McNamara, a family friend, visited three sites in Arlington National Cemetery, where America's war dead are buried, a mere two miles from the White House as the crow flies. Robert Kennedy chose Lot 45, Section 30, on a grassy slope below Arlington House, the home of Robert E. Lee, commander of the Confederate Army during the Civil War. The site had not previously been considered for burial because of the steepness of the slope. Mr. Kennedy and Secretary McNamara also visited Arlington House, where they were told that on a recent visit to the place, JFK had admired the view of Washington, D.C., and commented that he could enjoy it forever. That comment confirmed their choice of grave site, and Jacqueline Kennedy concurred.

Today Arlington House and the Kennedy grave site are at the terminus of an axis that runs across Memorial Bridge (a symbol of reconciliation between the North and the South) to the Lincoln Memorial and through the historic core of Washington, D.C.—past the Washington Monument and the statue of Ulysses S. Grant, Commanding General of the United States Army during the Civil War—and ending at the U.S. Capitol. By siting his brother's grave on this axial line, Robert Kennedy secured JFK's place in American history forever.

The funeral ceremonies took place on Saturday, Sunday, and Monday, November 23–25, in Washington, D.C. On Saturday the president's body lay in repose in the East Room, the largest public room in the White House and the setting for memorable musical performances by the likes of Leonard Bernstein, Pablo Casals, Igor Stravinsky, and Isaac Stern. The closed casket rested in the center of the room on the catafalque that had been used for Abraham Lincoln's funeral. At ten o'clock on Saturday morning a funeral mass was held in the State Dining Room.

On Sunday Kennedy's flag-covered casket was carried by horse-drawn caisson to the Capitol Rotunda, where the president's body would lie in state. On Monday the casket was moved to the Cathedral of St. Matthew the Apostle for a Requiem Mass at noon, followed by interment ceremonies at Arlington National Cemetery. That day was also John Jr.'s third birthday.

The Flower Room at the White House was located near the Rose Garden and next to the indoor swimming pool, where the president swam almost daily. The two florists, Elmer (Rusty) Young and James (Jimmy) Nelson, had often discussed flowers with the president. They kept a supply of purple bachelor buttons in the floral refrigerator for those occasions when the president chose to tuck one in his lapel.

On the evening of November 22, Jimmy and Rusty draped White House chandeliers and windows in memorial black crepe and began arranging flowers for the State Floor rooms in the airy, informal style that Mrs. Mellon had taught them. For the East Room they made two floral sprays of white flowers—daisies, chrysanthemums, lilies, carnations, and roses—to flank the casket. In a 1964 interview conducted by the first lady's press secretary, the florists were asked who had been in charge of the floral arrangements for the funeral. They replied, "Mrs. Mellon."

Mrs. Mellon had been in Antigua when the news of the president's assassination reached her. At 5:59 P.M. on November 23 she sent a telegram to Perry Wheeler that read, "Leaving on first plane today. Please give my love and thoughts to all we work with. Much love Bunny." She endured a storm-tossed return to Washington, D.C., a "journey something of an epic," as William Manchester described it in his book *The Death of a President*. Arriving at the White House late Saturday night, Bunny was met by chief usher J. B. West, who relayed Mrs. Kennedy's request for Bunny to arrange the flowers for the Rotunda at the Capitol, the church, and Arlington. At some point on Sunday, Mrs. Kennedy spoke directly with Bunny and said, as quoted by Sally Bedell Smith in her book *Grace and Power*, "I don't want the church to look like a funeral. . . . I want it like spring." Acknowledging the pleasure that the Rose Garden had brought the president, Mrs. Kennedy asked for "a straw basket with just the flowers he had in the Rose Garden. Only those flowers, and nothing else at the grave," and she suggested a personal touch, "In the bottom of the basket . . . somewhere scrunched down, put in your own note to Jack."

For the Capitol Rotunda, Rusty Young created a floral wreath that was placed near the casket. At Mrs. Mellon's request, two palm trees were borrowed from the U.S. Botanic Garden and placed at the Rotunda entrance. Floral tributes were displayed in an adjoining vestibule and later moved to Arlington, where Bunny had them spread on a nearby hillside "like an enormous blanket," according to Sally Bedell Smith.

For the church, Bunny filled two blue urns with simple arrangements of white daisies, chrysanthemums, and

stephanotis. November is late for flowers in Washington, D.C., but there were still dozens of white roses, some blue salvia, and chrysanthemums in the Rose Garden, as well as foliage from the hawthorn and crab apple trees. Bunny added these to a bouquet of nicotiana, red geraniums, carnations, and cornflowers nestled in a straw basket and tucked in her hand-written note, "Thank you Mr. President for your confidence and inspiration. Love, Bunny."

A few days after the funeral, Jacqueline Kennedy and Robert Kennedy returned to the grave site with family friend and architect John Carl Warnecke, of John Carl Warnecke and Associates, to discuss design concepts for a permanent resting place. Warnecke and partner-in-charge of landscape architecture, Michael Painter (today president of MPA Design), had recently completed the redesign of Lafayette Square across Pennsylvania Avenue from the White House, a project that Jacqueline Kennedy had spearheaded, and Warnecke had traveled with President Kennedy to Boston to scout potential locations

for the Kennedy Presidential Library. At the time, two decisions were made: the Kennedys' two deceased infants would be reinterred at their father's side and the flame that had been lighted at the graveside burial service would remain—eternally.

On November 30, 1963, the New York Times reported that John Carl Warnecke and Associates would design President Kennedy's tomb in Arlington. The design process was highly secretive. The firm began a study to determine the purpose of the site: was it to be a grave, a memorial, or a monument? They researched the history of Arlington National Cemetery, other presidential grave sites, and important tombs around the world. Warnecke consulted with dozens of architects, landscape architects, artists, sculptors, stonemasons, and calligraphers. The firm's seventy-six-page confidential report, "John F. Kennedy Memorial Grave: Design Reviews Concerning Sculpture and the Flame," completed in August 1964, concluded that the site would be a grave and identified two cardinal principles for the grave-site design: "First, the flame is the primary symbol at the grave, stronger than any sculpture or any structure that might be added to it. Second, the total design and composition must be simple, and out of its simplicity and dignity will come its beauty." Mrs. Kennedy expressed hope that there would be a definite plan soon.

In the first year after President Kennedy's death, more than five million people visited the temporary grave site. Accommodating such crowds on the steeply sloped hillside prompted Painter's design of a circular walkway that skirted a 150-year-old oak tree known as the "Arlington Oak."

On November 17, 1964, at the National Gallery of Art in Washington, D.C., Robert McNamara (who, as secretary of Defense, had jurisdiction over Arlington National Cemetery), John Warnecke, and members of the Kennedy family announced plans for the permanent grave site, which was to be built twenty feet downhill from the temporary grave. The permanent site would retain Painter's circular granite walkway; a low granite wall inscribed with excerpts from President Kennedy's inaugural address and other speeches would rim an elliptical marble plaza; from there, steps would lead up to a rectangular terrace, where the graves and the eternal flame would be located. The eternal flame would be held in a bronze brazier, and an eight-foot-high marble retaining wall engraved with the Presidential seal would be built at the rear of the site against the hillside. The final details of the rectangular grave site and landscaping had not been finalized. Warnecke expected construction to begin in the fall of 1965 and completed a year later.

Throughout the planning stages, Warnecke discussed the design with Mrs. Kennedy, and on February 17, 1964, he noted that the discussion had "come around to flowering trees." Remembering how much her husband had loved his White House garden and how beautiful it looked in the spring and fall, Mrs. Kennedy once again requested Mrs. Mellon's assistance.

The Mellon team reassembled: landscape architect Perry Wheeler—Bunny's eyes and ears; Irvin Williams, the White House gardener/diplomat and problem solver; tree expert Everett Hicks; and W. J. Hanback, the highly respected general contractor in Warrenton, Virginia, who had served as the contractor for Trinity Episcopal Church.

At first Mrs. Mellon's involvement was confined to the landscaping, and the search began for mature trees to create an immediate impact and blend with the cemetery's arboretum-like landscape—especially the 150-year-old Arlington Oak. As the design evolved, it became increasingly important to Mrs. Kennedy for her husband's grave site to blend in atmospherically with what she felt was a Civil War–era cemetery—and not obstruct, or compete with, the view of Arlington House.

On January 24, 1965, Winston Churchill, one of Kennedy's heroes, died. This "descendant of dukes and modern day hero who had rescued a democracy," as Mrs. Mellon described him, was buried in his family's country churchyard in a simple grave, with only his name and birth and death dates etched in stone. According to Painter, "Jacqueline Kennedy began to wonder if our design was too formal and architectural after hearing of the simplicity of Winston Churchill's grave."

Construction of the Kennedy grave site finally began in June 1965, and as the work progressed, the revisions continued. Warnecke decided to cover the rectangular terrace in fescue (a troublesome choice for Virginia's humid climate; it was liable to develop brown spots) and elevate the eternal flame instead of maintaining its low profile. The marble for the eight-foot-tall retaining wall had been quarried, cut, and fabricated and was ready to be shipped; and granite steps connecting the grave site to Arlington House were installed. As the granite and marble elements were taking shape, the grave site began to look more like the Tomb of the Unknown Soldier than a family grave. So in addition to selecting and positioning all the trees and shrubs, Mrs. Mellon was asked to complete the design for the rectangular terrace where the graves and the eternal flame would be located.

In her search for inspiration, Mrs. Mellon turned to history, first to the simple, tasteful grave sites of George Washington and Thomas Jefferson, and then to the memory of John F. Kennedy himself, a New Englander who had loved the sea, the out-of-doors, and the architectural traditions of the past. He had supported the effort to preserve Dolley Madison's home and the other Colonial-era buildings on Lafayette Square across from the White

House, and he had been involved in restoring that building too. He revered men of exceptional valor in American history, including the eight senators he celebrated in his Pulitzer Prize–winning book of essays, *Profiles in Courage*. When welcoming American Nobel Prize winners to the White House on April 29, 1962, President Kennedy remarked: "I think that this is the most extraordinary collection of talent, of human knowledge, that has ever been gathered together at the White House, with the possible exception of when Thomas Jefferson dined alone."

Mrs. Mellon felt that the very idea of a marble edifice would have been alien to President Kennedy. "Marble is for Emperors and is not the material of a democrat," she said. "Great men do not need huge tombs to show the world that they were great; rather, it is the other way around." She, of course, had gained firsthand knowledge of the president's small "d" democratic convictions when he asked for the steps leading from his office portico to the Rose Garden to be redesigned, requesting that the central step be enlarged into a speaking platform so that honorees could occupy the upper steps during ceremonies. He didn't want to tower over them.

Mrs. Mellon would have preferred for the grave site's marble steps to be removed but agreed to have them ground down to give them an aged look and create a subtle transition from the public area of the elliptical plaza to the graves on the rectangular terrace. She decided to border the rectangular terrace with a hedge of *Osmanthus fragrans*, reinforcing the sense of entering a sanctuary, and surround it with a small grove of trees that had been favorites of the president's: six *Magnolia* x *soulangeana*, four of which came from the same site as those planted in the Rose Garden, crab apple, willow oak, hawthorn, yellowwood, American beech, American holly, and autumn flowering cherry. Fescue was to be the principal ground cover for the lawn circumscribed by the circular walkway, and the great Arlington Oak would continue to dominate the site. Arlington House would remain in full view, the hillside undisturbed.

On the rectangular terrace, irregularly shaped slabs of Cape Cod granite were used instead of the proposed fescue. They were laid with exacting care. The graves were marked by three slate squares: the president's, his son Pat-

rick's, and his unnamed daughter's. Fescue, a bittersweet reminder of the president's concern about the grass in the Rose Garden, red clover, and Irish shamrock were sown in the crevices between the stones.

The pink Cape Cod granite is a symbolic reference to the president's home on Cape Cod. Reportedly, the Kennedys had admired the pretty pink stone at an antiques shop in West Falmouth on weekend outings. It had been quarried in that town in the 1800s. In the summer of 1966 Mrs. Mellon located a barn with a foundation of the pink stone and had it shipped to her Upperville farm, where Mr. Hanback's crew cut and chiseled it into irregularly shaped slabs, each of which was numbered and keyed to a diagram, so that, like jigsaw-puzzle pieces, they would fit perfectly on the terrace. Instead of a bronze brazier, a millstone of the same granite, set nearly flush with the ground, was used as a bracket for the eternal flame.

Everett Hicks began planting trees on Christmas Eve, 1966, and in January 1967 Perry Wheeler and Irv Williams were on site as two of the magnolias were planted on either side of the steps. It was a nostalgic moment for the two men. Afterward, Wheeler penned a note to Mrs. Mellon: "When the two magnolias went in on each side of the steps and Mr. Williams and I looked back toward the Lincoln Memorial—we both had the same feeling—it was so much like looking from just outside President Kennedy's office door under the same low branching limbs at the South Border of the Rose Garden."

By early February, Mr. Hanback and the stonemasons were nearing completion of their work on the stones that would cover the grave site. Before the graves were relocated, the circular stone bracket for the eternal flame was brought to the site. A technician from the Institute of Gas Technology in Chicago installed the gas nozzle and connected the electrical ignition and the compressed air and natural gas lines as the stone was being lowered into final position.

In March, as the tree planting continued, Everett Hicks devised a maintenance schedule that included regular pruning and a complete watering, fertilizing, and insect-control program.

On the evening of March 14, 1967, after the cemetery had closed, the grave site was illuminated for several hours and the caskets of the president and his infant son and daughter were reinterred in their final resting places. After the caskets were positioned and covered with earth, the Cape Cod granite was laid in Mrs. Mellon's perfect pattern. The temporary flame was extinguished and the eternal one was lighted. Robert and Edward Kennedy, with Secretary McNamara and Richard Cardinal Cushing, the Archbishop of Boston, stood watch until the final stone was in place.

At dawn the next morning, a brief consecration service was held in the rain. It was attended by Mrs. Kennedy, Mrs. Mellon, the Kennedy family, and President Johnson. The archbishop stood at the president's grave and gave a blessing: "Be at peace, dear Jack, with your tiny infants by your side, until we all meet again above the hill and beyond the stars."

Afterward, Mrs. Kennedy wrote to John Warnecke: "I went to Arlington. It will be beautiful—it is already. . . . It is exactly as I wish it and as I asked Bunny Mellon to make it—as if he had been laid to rest in his beloved Rose Garden that she made for him. . . ."

In the end, the design focused on the space, the sightlines, and the surrounding environs. The steps leading from the gravesite to Arlington House were considered an imposition on the hillside and demolished; the eight-foot retaining wall was never installed. These changes were not widely reported. Perhaps the press never knew or chose to keep quiet about them.

Another thing that was kept quiet was Mrs. Mellon's involvement in designing the rectangular terrace where the graves are located. Michael Painter said, "Mrs. Mellon designed the gravesite 100 percent and never received credit for her work." In an old family cemetery at Oak Spring there is a mock-up of the grave site: a large circular stone surrounded by irregularly shaped stones fitted perfectly together. Someone is remembered, but no one is buried there.

Jacqueline Kennedy Onassis was buried at her first husband's side on May 24, 1994. And today a sign reading "Silence and Respect" is posted at the entrance to the elliptical plaza. The inscribed words "Ask not what your country can do for you . . . " are fading from the low wall but not from our hearts or memories. A steady

{ KENNEDY FAMILY GARDENS }

stream of visitors somberly climbs the steps from the plaza to the grave site.

The green hedge and the *Magnolia* x *soulangeana* are still there. The crab apple bears its fruit in fall, and the autumn flowering cherries blossom in spring and fall. Painter said that Mrs. Mellon chose trees that would bloom through the seasons so there would always be something beautiful to see. The Arlington Oak, a victim of Hurricane Irene in 2011, was replaced by a sapling grown from one of its acorns. President Kennedy would be comforted to know that his devoted brothers are buried nearby, as is Thurgood Marshall, the first African American Supreme Court justice. And Mrs. Kennedy would be pleased to know that her husband's grave is still beautiful. Mrs. Mellon made it exactly as she wished.

PAGE 260: A circular millstone brackets the eternal flame on the rectangular grave site, paved with Cape Cod granite.

PAGE 261: The grave-site terrace is located down a steep slope from Arlington House. Slate squares mark the graves of John F. Kennedy and Jacqueline Kennedy Onassis.

PAGE 263: Jacqueline Kennedy, accompanied by family and friends, places flowers on her husband's grave

PAGES 266–67: The grave site is on an axis that begins at Arlington House and runs across Memorial Bridge to the Lincoln Memorial.

LEFT: To this day, the magnolias that Bunny planted grace the grave-site terrace as visitors file by to pay their respects to the president.

ABOVE: Bunny's mock-up of the Kennedy grave site in an old family cemetery at Oak Spring.

JOHN F. KENNEDY PRESIDENTIAL LIBRARY AND MUSEUM

When it was time for Jacqueline Kennedy to review the landscape drawings and plans for the John F. Kennedy Presidential Library and Museum, she brought her friend Bunny Mellon along. And a familiar scenario ensued. • The landscape drawings had been prepared by Daniel Urban Kiley of Kiley, Tyndall, Walker for I. M. Pei, the architect of the presidential library. Pei had originally been commissioned in 1964 to design the building on a site adjacent to Harvard University in Cambridge. But after years of delays and setbacks, he and his associate, Theodore Musho, started over with a new design on a 9½-acre site at Columbia Point, a former landfill overlooking Dorchester Bay and the Atlantic Ocean, with panoramic views of

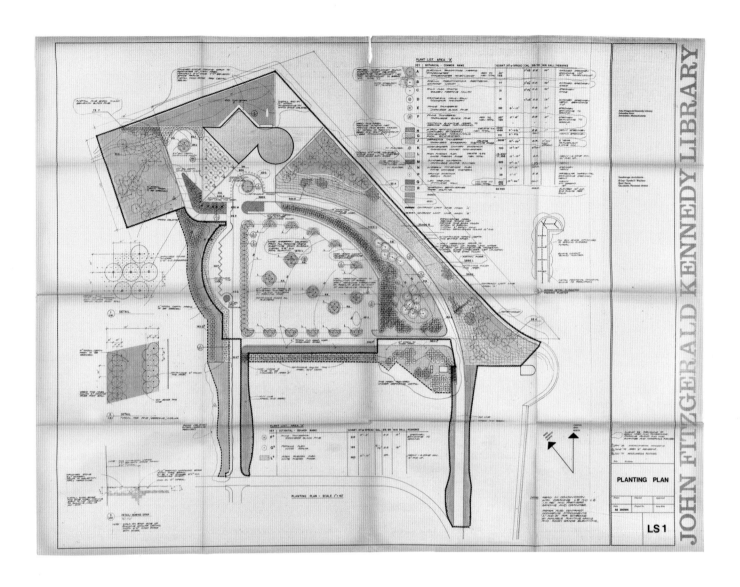

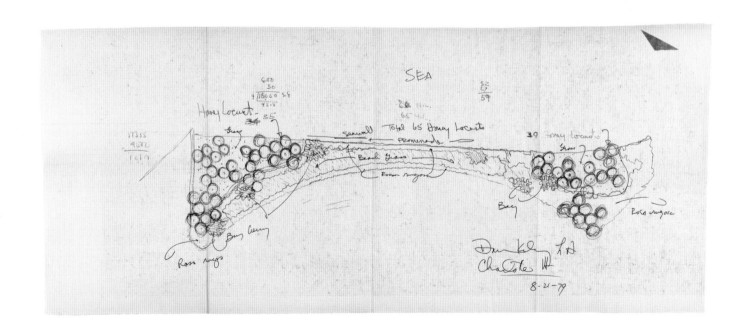

{ KENNEDY FAMILY GARDENS }

Boston's skyline, a setting that evokes JFK's love of sailing and the sea. Their mission was to create a complex that was both contemporary and timeless, a reflection of the former president's youthfulness and legendary appeal.

Dan Kiley, a noted landscape architect whose work included the landscaping of the Air Force Academy in Colorado Springs, Colorado; the Jefferson National Expansion Memorial in St. Louis, Missouri; La Défense, a business district just west of Paris; and the East Wing of the National Gallery in Washington, D.C., had applied his approach of uniting the architecture with the site through his design to the presidential library project. Mrs. Mellon took one look at his landscape drawings and remarked, "I always thought of the president as a wind man." And she suggested planting beach grass and *Rosa rugosa* along the curving road leading to the main entrance to the library.

When interviewed about this meeting for an oral history in 2002, Musho recalled his surprise at Mrs. Mellon's comment: "A wind man. Holy mackerel! . . . But it made absolutely perfect sense because she's the one that thought of that dune grass out on the curb. . . . To a point from when it was built to, I would say, five, six years out, that dune grass moved with the wind. Then the rosa rugose [sic], which was behind it, created this aroma. When you drove up that path, or preferably got out of your car and walked up that curve, the aroma of that rosa rugose with that wind moving this grass, it was absolutely magic." Even Dan Kiley, who was at the meeting, "flipped" when he heard her remark. They found her "electric."

Musho also recalled that when the president's brother-in-law Steve Smith, chairman of the John F. Kennedy Library Corporation, who wasn't at the meeting, heard that their landscaping plan had been trashed, he exclaimed, "Mrs. Mellon had another one!" But he immediately understood her reason for suggesting the beach grass and the *Rosa rugosa*, both of which grow abundantly on the dunes along the coastline of the president's beloved Cape Cod.

Dan Kiley collaborated with Mrs. Mellon to create a new landscape plan. Beach grass, beach plum, bayberry, and white *Rosa rugosa* were planted along one side of the curved drive. Rows of Japanese black pines were planted on the opposite side. Viewed from the front entrance, the

drive, lined with the combination of the *Rosa rugosa* and the grass bending in the wind, carries the observer's eye to the sea. To the northeast of the drive is an embankment—a 1,000-foot lawn that gradually slopes down to Dorchester Bay. Groves of honey locusts underplanted with lawn grass provide windbreaks on both sides of the embankment. At the foot of the embankment, a walkway extends along a seawall that is punctuated with white concrete bollards and a weighty chain, imparting a maritime atmosphere.

The drive ends in a circle at the main entrance of the library building, where it connects to a parking lot shaded by clusters of Shademaster honey locusts underplanted with white *Rosa rugosa*. To the northwest, a grove of weeping willows underplanted with lawn grass provides a shady picnic area for visitors.

Interviewed for an article in the *New York Times* about Bunny Mellon entitled "The Private World of a Great Gardener," I. M. Pei recalled their collaboration on the presidential library and offered his opinion of her skill as a landscape designer: "Mrs. Mellon has the combination of sensitivity and imagery with technical knowledge that you only find among the best professionals."

PAGES 268–69: Front façade of the John F. Kennedy Presidential Library and Museum, designed by I. M. Pei.

PAGE 270 TOP: The landscape plan for the presidential library grounds, based on Bunny's recommendations.

PAGE 270 BOTTOM: Bunny's landscape plan for the lawn along Dorchester Bay.

PAGE 271: The windswept dune grass Bunny suggested planting along the curving road leading to the main entrance.

ABOVE: JFK's boat, the *Victura*, faces Dorchester Bay and the Boston skyline.

BELOW: The bollard-lined walkway along Dorchester Bay.

RIGHT: The approach to the entrance of the John F. Kennedy Presidential Library and Museum.

Gardens in France

CHÂTEAU DU JONCHET, EURE-ET-LOIR

On a memorable day in 1968, Bunny Mellon's longtime couturier, Cristóbal Balenciaga, announced to her that he was retiring, and walked her across Avenue George V to the atelier of his protégé Hubert de Givenchy. That introduction marked the beginning not only of a new designer-client relationship but also of a deep and abiding friendship. Sharing a profound admiration for the horticultural traditions of the past, in time they collaborated on the redesign and restoration of several historic French gardens. • In the early days of her association with Givenchy, Bunny placed an order for one hundred dresses. "I called her office to ask if this was correct. It was," Givenchy recalled. And when he found out that she had ordered the same dress in multiple colors for different houses—and climates—it made perfect sense to him. He was impressed with her efficiency. • In a departure from couture tradition, Givenchy conducted Bunny's fittings himself, and during the fittings, they would have wide-ranging discussions about art and

fashion, houses, décor, and gardening. Their conversations would go on and on until Bunny would finally say, "Hubert, get back to the hem!"

Bunny's wardrobe suited a lifestyle that called for comfort and ease of movement—an elegant simplicity. Givenchy fondly remembered her particular affinity for "what is it called in America . . . blue jean!" He designed denim skirts, hats, tops, and raincoats for her "working gardener" attire.

Bunny once spotted a hat in the fitting room and asked to buy it. "Of course you can," Givenchy recalled telling her. "You may have anything in the shop that you want, but will you please allow me to make you a dress to go with the hat? The hat is an accessory." But all she wanted was the hat—she was taken with its fine craftsmanship. Givenchy was inspired by this attitude. "That was Bunny. Such a keen eye she had—and seeing beautiful lines gave her such joy."

In 1975 Givenchy acquired a country house, the sixteenth-century Château du Jonchet, located in the Eure-et-Loir department, southwest of Paris. Together, the two collaborators cast their spell over the 224-acre park, transforming it into gardens that even Louis XIV would have admired.

Bunny had studied the methods and techniques of the great gardeners of France. Two of her favorites were André Le Nôtre, who designed the gardens at Vaux-le-Vicomte and Versailles, among others, and Jean-Baptiste de La Quintinie, who created potagers (kitchen gardens) for Anne Marie Louise d'Orléans, known as the Grande Mademoiselle; Louis II, Prince de Condé; Charles de Sainte-Maure, duc de Montausier; Nicolas Fouquet at Vaux-le-Vicomte; and Versailles. Louis XIV appointed La Quintinie director of the first potager at Versailles in 1661 and later administrator of the fruit trees and potagers on all of the royal estates.

The purpose of these gardens and potagers was two-fold: to enhance the beauty of the architecture through the skillful establishment of sightlines with extensive vistas beyond property boundaries and to increase fruit and vegetable production through superior cultivation methods. Bunny applied Le Nôtre's theories of landscape design and La Quintinie's ideas on fruit and vegetable production in her creation of the gardens and potager at Château du Jonchet.

The château and the four towers at the corners of its courtyard are encircled by a water-filled moat, complete with a drawbridge and graceful swans, and surrounded by dense forest, open fields, and waterways—a storied setting for a fairy-tale enthusiast like Bunny Mellon to work her magic.

Along the length of the entrance façade, she placed a series of trees in planters to soften the stone wall, but she refrained from any plantings at the foundation, feeling that they would detract from the château's pure lines. A broad path extends from the entrance through the courtyard. Flanking it are squares of meticulously manicured lawn—three on each side—perhaps inspired by the lawns at the entrance to Vaux-le-Vicomte. Punctuating the four corners of each square are circular, flat-topped bushes, suggesting buttons. Mounted over the entrance, and presiding over the courtyard, are three carved-stone stag heads. Stag imagery is found throughout the château, both outside and in, appearing as sculptures and weathervanes, mounted above fireplaces, embroidered on pillows, and even etched into glassware. Hubert is the name of the patron saint of hunters, and his emblem is the stag. Although Givenchy did not hunt, he appreciated the dynamic sculptural quality of antlers.

The path crosses over the moat and ends at a series of steps that descends through an opening in an imposing hornbeam hedge to a large, geometrically patterned greensward. Boxwood hedges outline squares and rectangles, within which swirl large concentric circles and smaller circles, also formed of boxwood hedges. Surrounding this lawn is a high, whitewashed stone wall that is bordered with hedges, beds of flowers and shrubs, fruit trees, and water features. Givenchy credited the inspiration for the geometric design of the lawn to the cloister of the

PAGES 276–77: Italian inspiration with a French twist: boxwood hedges are planted in geometric shapes on the velvety green lawn at Château du Jonchet.

PAGE 278: A row of stag-head sculptures embellishes the château entrance.

PAGE 279: Images of stags, the symbol of St. Hubert—patron saint of hunters and Givenchy's saint's name—are found all over the property.

PAGE 280: An aerial view of the château: The formal gardens evoke the classical designs of André Le Nôtre.

PAGE 281: "Because of those tall windows, light itself seems like an architectural mass formed with love. I adore that façade," Givenchy once said.

PAGES 282–83: The courtyard entrance of Château du Jonchet, featuring the button-like bushes at the corners of the manicured squares of lawn.

PAGE 284 TOP: A stag head decorates a wall.

PAGE 284 BOTTOM: Another stag head embellishes a stone pier.

PAGE 285, CLOCKWISE FROM TOP LEFT: Stone steps lead through a perfectly clipped hornbeam hedge to the expansive lawn; a topiary chair adds a bit of whimsy to the beds bordering the lawn; a white bench is an inviting spot to view the lawn; a statue provides a focal point in the border framing the lawn.

LEFT: Boxwood hedges in concentric circles within rectangles give texture to the lawn.

PAGES 288–89: The inspiration for the geometric design of the lawn was the cloister of the seventeenth-century Benedictine Monastery of San Giorgio Maggiore in Venice,

PAGES 290–91: A sundial balances a gardener's house directly across the lawn.

seventeenth-century Benedictine Monastery of San Giorgio Maggiore in Venice, Italy. Ever a man of integrity, Givenchy journeyed to the monastery to seek the monks' permission to replicate the design at his château.

Beyond the lawn, the Aigre River, a tributary of the Loir, flows into an artfully shaped lake at the far end of the property. It serves as a focal point of the view from the château. A wattle fence creates a basket-like border around the perimeter of the lake, a literal evocation of *jonchet*, which means "stick" or "reed."

Givenchy and Bunny infused the château gardens with touches of whimsy. They marked the shadow cast by a large tree, aptly nicknamed the "Great Shadow," and planted it with hundreds of blue scilla. "This surprise of lapis blue in the grass lasting only two weeks each year had a magical quality. And the blue multiplied, becoming bluer each year," Bunny noted in her journal. "A house of this structure, period and noblesse cannot have flowered borders in evidence." It was better for drifts of narcissus, violets, and other woodland plants to appear in swaths under trees.

In the course of working on the landscaping, Bunny reached the conclusion that a portion of the forest near the château had to be cleared. Givenchy recalled the conversation they had about it: "Hubert, the stand of trees is blocking the view. It has to be taken down," she told him. "What?" he exclaimed, "Take down the forest?" "Yes," she insisted, "It is a problem." Givenchy told her he'd think about it, and, despite his inclination to always heed her advice, he chose to leave the stand of trees as it was. Bunny later returned to the subject—she had reconsidered. "No, Hubert, the trees should stay." Givenchy was greatly relieved, "I was so happy the trees were still there! Can you imagine what it would have cost to replant all those trees?! Incredible. I told Bunny, 'We must go slowly.'"

On one of Givenchy's trips to the United States, Bunny introduced him to the gardens and grounds at Mount Vernon, George and Martha Washington's plantation on the Potomac River in Virginia. The two friends found fresh inspiration in the Upper and Lower Gardens, the former a pleasure garden filled with flowers, and the latter a utilitarian one planted with fruits, herbs, and vegetables. Givenchy decided to create a Mount Vernon–style

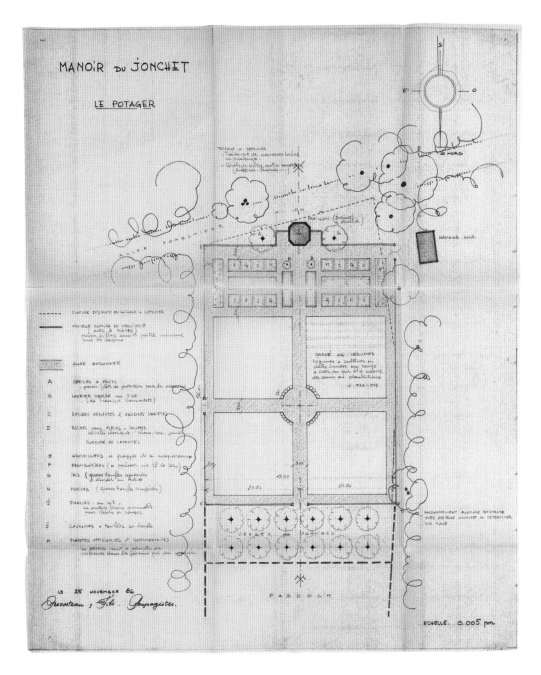

kitchen garden—a potager—at Jonchet. The old had become new again.

Before proceeding, they consulted their "Bible," *The Compleat Gard'ner: or, Directions for Cultivating and Right Ordering of Fruit-Gardens, and Kitchen-Gardens* by Monsieur de La Quintinie. Understanding that a garden is "like a piece of cloth and is woven of numerous threads," Bunny wanted to be absolutely sure that the new garden would reflect Givenchy's persona and the setting of Château du Jonchet.

The plans for the potager, formalized on January 9, 1988, specified four square beds demarcated by two perpendicular grass paths running north–south and east–west; two matching garden houses in the southeast and southwest corners, with a grid of square and rectangular flower beds between them; a grove of trees on the southern end; and an apple orchard on the northern end. A white rail fence resembling one at Mount Vernon enclosed the garden.

The four square beds were planted with a great variety of flowers and vegetables in what Givenchy described as a "combined harmony." To this day, the rotating selection of vegetables includes asparagus, broccoli, Brussels sprouts, cabbages, celeriac, chard, chervil, chives, dill, haricots verts, leeks, lettuces, onions, melons, parsley, peas, potatoes, shallots, and tomatoes. The borders are embroidered like the trim of a dress with the purple blooms and tantalizing fragrance of lavender, the moody grays of santolina, and the green (Givenchy's favorite color) and white shoots of asparagus. "I dress the garden with a new look each season—just like a collection," Givenchy once said.

One of the two Mount Vernon–style garden houses, or "pavilions," as Givenchy called them, is reserved for the head gardener. The other was Givenchy's exclusive domain, styled with American practicality and an aesthetic of yesteryear: straw baskets (metal makes such a clanging noise), books, cushioned chairs, hand-tooled trowels, quilts, watering cans, and a wood-burning fireplace. "Each little thing in my pavilion comes from a trip and is something I love," Givenchy told visitors.

For decades Givenchy bewitched the fashion world with his deft manipulations of fabric on the human form, and he did likewise in his collaboration with Mrs. Mellon on the potager. The beds between the two pavilions are filled with flowers of the season planted in groups: peonies, irises, dahlias and other annuals, santolina, and classic varieties of roses.

Behind the pavilions, a serpentine walk threads through a grove of trees, including Bigarreau sweet cherry, quince, Reine Claude Verte plum, Mirabelle de Nancy plum, Quetsche d'Alsace plum, Montmorency cherry, myrtle, Mahonia, oak, maple, blackthorn, hawthorn, hazel, holly, and walnut, as well as raspberry, gooseberry, black currant, and blackberry bushes.

In the apple orchard at the opposite end of the potager, the trees are planted in two straight rows on a swath of lawn. A curved wooden bench, partially shaded, provides respite from the afternoon sun and a view of the orchard for contemplation.

{ GARDENS IN FRANCE }

POTAGER DU ROI, VERSAILLES

*"Jean de la Quintinie, the genius who created
the Potager du Roi and whose methods and
understanding of growing fruit and vegetables
were 300 years ahead of his time, was a respected
and beloved friend of the king."*

—RACHEL LAMBERT MELLON,
OAK SPRING, APRIL 1993

The Potager du Roi, the king's kitchen garden at the Palace of Versailles, was created between 1678 and 1686 by Jean-Baptiste de La Quintinie and the architect Jules Hardouin-Mansart to supply the dining tables of the court of Louis XIV with delicious fruits and vegetables. La Quintinie was a visionary in the development of techniques to harvest fruit in and out of season. He recorded his methods of fruit and vegetable production in his book *Instruction pour les jardins fruitiers et potagers*, which was published in 1690, two years after his death, and translated into English in 1693 by John Evelyn as *The Compleat Gard'ner*: "I succeeded in making some ripen five or six weeks early. For example strawberries in March and peas in April." At the royal court the peas were a huge success. Madame de Sévigné wrote in a letter, "The craze for peas continues; the impatience of waiting to eat them, to have eaten them and the pleasure of eating them are the three subjects our princes have been discussing for the past four days."

Today the potager covers more than twenty-three acres and consists of twenty-eight small beds surrounding the Grand Carré, or large square, which is divided into sixteen beds. At the center of Grand Carré is a fountain in a circular basin. High stone walls enclose the potager and divide the smaller gardens, providing protection from harsh weather conditions and creating microclimates for maximizing fruit and vegetable production both in and out of season. The beds are planted with vegetables and fruit trees espaliered in the method that La Quintinie documented in his handbook. In Louis XIV's day, the fruit trees included fifty varieties of pears and twenty varieties of apples. The king had a special fondness for figs, so La Quintinie cultivated more than seven hundred fig trees, some of which bore fruit as early as mid-June, enabling the gardener to supply the king's table year round. Along the western side of the Grand Carré is a broad, elevated terrace, from which Louis XIV and his entourage could observe the garden operations. Upon La Quintinie's death in 1688, the king wrote to his widow, "Madame, we have both suffered an irreplaceable loss."

After Givenchy retired as a couturier in the mid-1990s, he accepted the presidency of the World Monuments Fund France, the mission of which is to protect and restore historical French sites. At the top of his list was the restoration of the Potager du Roi, which was in a state of decay, and for this he needed to enlist the talents of his American friend.

He and Bunny first visited the potager at twilight on a chilly autumn day as a mist was rising. The two friends walked along pathways lined with towering fruit trees espaliered on crumbling stone walls. "Trellises outlined beds of vegetables—row upon row of red and green cabbages, artichokes, blue green leeks, beets, and the feathered tops of carrots," Bunny recalled in "Mrs. Mellon's Secret Garden," an article she wrote for *House & Garden* in 1988. They passed by remnants of the central basin, explored tunnels hundreds of years old and littered with ancient gardening implements—harvest baskets, wheelbarrows, and watering vessels—and finally reached the King's Gate, forged by Alexis Fordrin in 1681 and the only original wrought-iron gate still extant at Versailles. Topped by the monogram of Louis XIV, it was the gate that the king passed through

every time he visited his potager—and his gardener. After that first visit Bunny wrote, "It was an astonishing experience to be led into this garden of fruit trees trained against walls and trellises often reaching heights of twenty feet with a few pears still clinging to the trees."

Inspired by the traces of the potager's former glory and hoping to generate renewed interest in the garden, Mrs. Mellon wrote a letter to Jean-Pierre Babelon, at the time the director of the Museum and the National Domain of Versailles and Trianon, on June 2, 1990, in which she said, "We have ideas and hope to bring the garden back, with thought and time." She and Givenchy began to plan its restoration. They consulted La Quintinie's handbook and visited other châteaux with important fruit and vegetable gardens, including Vaux-le-Vicomte, where La Quintinie had planted a potager for the king's finance minister, Nicolas Fouquet, and Château de Villandry in the Loire Valley, renowned for its elaborate formal gardens and extensive potager. Mrs. Mellon also spent hours in the Potager du Roi

with the French gardeners, learning French pruning techniques and no doubt practicing her French language skills. In September 1990 she commissioned a scale model of the Potager du Roi as it had appeared in the seventeenth century.

When their site visits and research were completed, Mrs. Mellon and Givenchy drew up a comprehensive plan for the restoration of the central basin with its fountain, the irrigation system, and the King's Gate. As fundraising for the project got underway, Givenchy recalled, Bunny shared the following conversation with him: "Paul and I were having drinks as we do in the evening and I said, 'Paul, do you know Hubert de Givenchy?' And Paul said, 'Of course I know Hubert.' "Well, he's looking for some money to make repairs to the basin at the Potager du Roi. Do you think we could make a contribution?"

"The next afternoon," Givenchy continued, "I received a message from Bunny saying she and Paul would pay for the entire basin! I told her we must make a plaque to honor you and Mr. Mellon and she said, 'No, we

PAGE 298: The fully restored King's Gate, through which Louis XIV accessed the Potager du Roi.

PAGES 300–1: The Potager du Roi as it looks today, with the restored basin at the center of the sixteen-bed Grand Carré.

ABOVE: The gardeners at the Potager du Roi harvest fruit from the espaliered apple trees.

OPPOSITE: St. Louis Cathedral looms large behind the student gardens at the Potager du Roi.

don't want any attention.' 'But, I must acknowledge your generosity! I need to tell where the money came from. I don't want to go to jail!' 'Ah, oh okay,' she said. 'You can do that. But very small and unobtrusive.'"

A plaque in English and French attached to the ledge of the basin reads:

This basin has been restored by the kindness of Paul Mellon in Honor of Rachel Lambert Mellon with Appreciation for Her Love of The Potager du Roi.
WORLD MONUMENTS FUND
FRANCE—1996

When the restoration was complete, Bunny presented the scale model of the Potager du Roi to the Palace of Versailles. And on January 26, 1995, in gratitude for her contribution to the restoration, the French Ministry of Culture named her an Officier de l'Ordre des Arts et des Lettres.

In the summer of 1996 a benefit dinner was held in the garden to honor the Mellons, celebrate the completion of the restoration, and raise the garden's profile. On her arrival, Mrs. Mellon received a standing ovation from the gardeners, which touched her deeply. They presented her with a photograph of the garden that is on display in the library of the Oak Spring Garden Foundation. She and Givenchy were also given keys to the newly restored gate.

Since 1995 le the Potager du Roi has been under the stewardship of the École Nationale Supérieure de Paysage (French National Landscape Architecture School). Antoine Jacobsohn, the current director of the potager, oversees the planting, pruning, and harvesting of hundreds of varieties of fruits and vegetables, and supervises experiments with cultivation techniques. Through Jacobsohn's efforts, the Potager du Roi is once again on the World Monuments Fund Watch list "to address a number of challenges, including damaged and outdated drainage systems, greenhouses, supporting structures, and amenities for visitors," as the fund's website states. Particularly vulnerable are the deteriorating stone walls that support the espaliered fruit trees. On a recent tour of the potager, Antoine Jacobsohn exclaimed, "We need Mrs. Mellon today!" And though there was only one Bunny Mellon, the search is on for someone who will care as deeply about and do as much to further the mission of this important, precious garden of the past—and the future.

For Irvin Williams,
White House Gardener

"Everything about Mr. Williams is nice; he was just a
dream to work with and we had perfect rapport.
He was influential in helping me to create new gardens."
—Bunny Mellon, 2010

ACKNOWLEDGMENTS

With my deepest gratitude to the following people for their confidence in me and belief in this book and for sharing their expertise, memories, and precious time:

The late Rachel Lambert Mellon, Irvin Williams, Sir Peter Crane, Mark Magowan, and Jacqueline Decter.

Oak Spring gardeners: Head Gardener Randy Embrey, Laura Booth, Deborah Byrd, Kate Cliffton, Airynee Damewood, Desiree Lee, Wendi Sirat, and J. D. Tutwiler. Oak Spring stonemason: Tommy Reed. Oak Spring librarians: Nancy Collins, Kimberley L. H. Fisher, Ricky Willis, and Tony Willis. Oak Spring multimedia production & communications associate: Max Smith.

Cape Cod gardeners: Lisa Rockwell, Chris Harvie, and Bob Hoxie.

Nantucket gardener: Neil Paterson.

Rev. Robert Banse, Mrs. Charles (Martha) Bartlett, Louise Beit, Mrs. William (Deeda) Blair, Max Blumberg, Gray Coyner, Betsy Crenshaw, Patty Fabricant, Alex Forger, the late Hubert de Givenchy, Jacques de Givry, W. Cabell Grayson, Maryrose Grossman, Daniel L. Haney, Margaret Harman, J. David Holden Jr., Bryan Huffman, Antoine Jacobsohn, Burt Kaplan, James F. Lentowsky, Thomas Lloyd, Jane MacLennan, Rachel Miller, Jim Morris, Dean Norton, Michael Painter, Katie Rainier, Jim Spivey, Draza Stamenich, Daniel Sutherland, Karen Tees, Steve Tees, Philippe Venet, Katherine Grayson Wilkins, the John F. Kennedy Presidential Library and Museum, and the LBJ Presidential Library and Museum.

Linda Jane Holden

INDEX

The Gardens of Bunny Mellon
First published in 2018 by The Vendome Press
Vendome is a registered trademark of The Vendome Press LLC

VENDOME PRESS US
PO Box 566
Palm Beach, FL 33480

VENDOME PRESS UK
Worlds End Studio
132-134 Lots Road
London, SW10 0RJ

www.vendomepress.com

Distributed in North America by Abrams Books
Distributed in the United Kingdom, and the rest of the world,
by Thames & Hudson

ISBN 978-0-86565-351-1

PUBLISHERS: Beatrice Vincenzini, Mark Magowan,
and Francesco Venturi
EDITOR: Jacqueline Decter
PRODUCTION DIRECTOR: Jim Spivey
PRODUCTION COLOR MANAGER: Dana Cole
DESIGNER: Patricia Fabricant

Oak Spring Garden Plan created by Max Smith

Library of Congress Cataloging-in-Publication Data
available upon request

Printed and bound in China by 1010 Printing International Ltd.
Sixth printing

PAGE 1: In the Oak Spring Garden Library, one of Bunny Mellon's hats
hangs above a chair she purchased in France.

PAGES 2–3: The gate in the southwest corner of the Formal Garden
at Oak Spring.

PAGE 4: Bunny Mellon overlooking a few of the little herb trees that
she loved to cultivate and prune.

PAGE 6: The branches of a flowering crab apple tree arch over the
southwest entrance gate, which opens onto the Upper Terrace in
the Formal Garden.

PHOTO CREDITS